"Jesus' final prayer with his discipl  thing: that we his followers demon; will both convict and attract the wat deep division, this book shows how to do exactly that."

Philip Yancey
Author of *What's So Amazing About Grace*

"Creed and community remind me that changing habits is hard, and practicing solidarity involves wrestling with my own failures. But, with the help of others, each one of us can mend the fault lines in our own lives and lend our hands to repair the world. Read these essays and discover you are not alone. You have friends, co-workers, mentors, and guides for the way."

Diana Butler Bass
Author of *Freeing Jesus, Grateful,* and *Grounded*

"A brilliant and loving collection of real stories, *How to Heal Our Divides* shows what brave, humble people are doing all over the world to heal hurt and build bridges to restoration and peace. With inspiration on every page – written by some of the world's most renowned authors – here's a source of hope and healing that arrives just when we need it most."

Patricia Raybon
Award-winning author of *My First White Friend: Reflections on Race, Love and Forgiveness* and *Undivided: A Muslim Daughter, Her Christian Mother, Their Path to Peace*

"This volume brings together a diverse team of creative practitioners of un-division. All of these practitioners are translating peace-making theory into practice on the street, in the neighborhood, and in the human heart. Not only that, but they are developing and revising theory through their practice. That's what makes each contribution so powerful."

Brian McLaren
Author of *Faith After Doubt: Why Your Beliefs Stopped Working and What to Do About It*

"Wow, what a beautiful collection of humans who offer and call us to wrestle with the complexity of what it will take to find healing and wholeness as individuals and communities. *How to Heal Our Divides* does not offer false promises of a guaranteed linear progression towards healing, but an invitation to see that healing will only come about when we can fully and truly see that our collective paths are fueled by risking the unknown, unexpected, and possible."

Bruce Reyes-Chow
Author of *In Defense of Kindness: Why It Matters, How It Changes Our Lives, and How It Can Save the World*

"For twenty-five years, the Center for Courage & Renewal has helped people reclaim the wholeness that is everyone's birthright gift, so they can bring their identity and integrity more fully into their personal, vocational, and public lives. I am happy to participate in *How to Heal Our Divides* to come alongside other organizations working with similar goals."

Parker J. Palmer
Founder and Senior Partner Emeritus
of the Center for Courage & Renewal

"A vast book of diverse and accessible ideas the world needs right now!"

Mark Schaefer
Author of *Cumulative Advantage*

"Filled with strong and hopeful voices, How to Heal Our Divides is a book that recognizes it will take more than a Kumbaya moment to bring wholeness to our society. It does the hard work of bringing civil discourse to the page in a way that shows us it is possible to talk even when we don't agree. The healing will begin from there."

Sophfronia Scott
Author of *The Seeker and the Monk: Everyday Conversations with Thomas Merton*

"Projects like the ones in this book are healing the world. My own work as an activist has been shaped by stories like the ones in this book. This is holy work we are doing. It begins with humility."

Shane Claiborne
Leader of Red Letter Christians

"Stark divisions tear asunder the Body of Christ, our political life, our cultural fabric, our economic life, and the global family. Healing those divisions is imperative for any hope of a sustainable, shared future. This book doesn't just say this is necessary. It shows how it is being done in concrete stories close to the ground."

Wesley Granberg-Michaelson
Author of *Without Oars: Casting Off into a Life of Pilgrimage* and former General Secretary Reformed Church in America

"The courageous work of antiracists engaged in the ongoing struggle for racial liberation saves lives. Literally. The work of the diverse organizations highlighted in this volume, and many others who are not, is vitally important."

Michael W. Waters
Award-winning author, professor, activist, social commentator, and the founder and Lead Pastor of Abundant Life A.M.E. Church in Dallas, Texas

"*How to Heal Our Divides* is a desperately needed book in these troubled times. Its pages are full of stories of people who are pursuing justice and healing through a wide variety of creative initiatives. If you're discouraged by the state of the world, this book will bring you hope, inspiration, and ideas for how you too can become a peacemaker."

Lori Erickson
Author of *Holy Rover* and *Near the Exit*

"There is a time and a season for both advocacy and activism. Both approaches are crucial to creating lasting change in our world and to following a radical rabbi who engaged in both activism and advocacy throughout his ministry. Christians should always be seeking to raise our voice and build relationships across divides – because this is how we will transform the world."

Rev. Brandan Robertson

Noted author, activist, and public theologian, working at the intersections of spirituality and social renewal

"Now, more than ever, we need thoughtful practitioners who are modeling imaginative, innovative and collaborative ways of healing the divides and renewing our shared commitment to the common good. This resource features some of the most trusted thought-leaders and change-makers of our generation who are engaged in the daily work of shaping a just and compassionate world for generations to come."

Mark Feldmeir

Author of *A House Divided: Engaging the Issues Through the Politics of Compassion*

"*How to Heal Our Divides* is an antidote to the poison of division that is bringing civilization to its knees. Its wide ranging and courageous collection of voices of reason and compassion comprise a call for action rooted in fresh thinking about and daring reimagining of what it can be to be human in the 21st century. Don't just read this book; live it."

Rabbi Rami Shapiro

Director, One River Foundation for the Preservation and Promotion of Perennial Wisdom

"If you are looking for hope in our polarized times, you must read *How to Heal Our Divides*. The peacemakers in this book offer their unique, real-world, practical solutions to heal our broken world. At a time when we only hear too much from those seeking to divide us, this book reminds us that many leaders are out there trying their best to act justly, love mercy and walk humbly with God."

Rev. Rich Tafel
Pastor, Church of the Holy City, Washington DC

"The Mission of the Absalom Jones Center for Racial Healing is to provide tools and experiences that allow faith communities – and the larger community of individuals – to engage in dismantling racism through education, prayer, dialogue, pilgrimage, and spiritual formation. We appreciate the opportunity to participate in *How to Heal Our Divides* to help spread the word about the work of the many outstanding organizations featured in the book."

Dr. Catherine Meeks
Executive Director of the Absalom Jones Center for Racial Healing

"The Better Arguments Project is a national civic initiative created to help bridge divides – not by papering over those divides but by helping Americans have better arguments. We appreciate the opportunity to participate in *How to Heal Our Divides* to illuminate the many ways in which organizations are effectively working to improve our country's civil discourse."

Seth Henderson
Program Manager at the Aspen Institute's Citizenship and American Identity Program

"*How to Heal Our Divides* is a timely toolkit for building bridges with empathy and action. Through compelling narratives and accessible wisdom from the authors, theologians, activists, advocates, and allies living this work, this encouraging book deserves many readers."

J. Dana Trent
Professor of Critical Thinking and World Religions
Author of *Saffron Cross: The Unlikely Story of How a Christian Minister Married a Hindu Monk*

How to Heal Our Divides

HOW TO HEAL OUR DIVIDES

A PRACTICAL GUIDE

COMPILED AND EDITED BY

BRIAN ALLAIN & ADAM THOMAS

Copyright © 2021 by Brian Allain

All rights reserved.

Authors contributing to this work are the sole owners of their contribution, and retain all rights to their contribution, except as granted to the publisher of this book, or except as otherwise noted herein. The publisher of this book is the sole owner of any rights associated with the book as a collective work.

ISBN 979-8-7457-8428-6

Scripture quotations marked (NIV) are taken from THE HOLY BIBLE, NEW INTERNATIONAL VERSION®, NIV® Copyright © 1973, 1978, 1984, 2011 by Biblica, Inc.™ Used by permission. All rights reserved worldwide.

Scripture quotations marked (NLT) are taken from the Holy Bible, New Living Translation, copyright © 1996, 2004, 2007 by Tyndale House Foundation. Used by permission of Tyndale House Publishers, Inc., Carol Stream, IL 60188. All rights reserved.

Scripture quotations marked (NRSV) are from the New Revised Standard Version Bible, copyright © 1989 the Division of Christian Education of the National Council of the Churches of Christ in the United States of America. Used by permission. All rights reserved.

Book design by Adam Thomas
adamthomas.net

To contact the publisher, please visit
howtohealourdivides.com

CONTENTS

PART ONE

WHY THIS MATTERS

HEALING OUR DIVIDES: WHY THIS MATTERS

Brian D. McLaren

In 2017, I was invited to get involved with Vote Common Good, led by my long-time friend Doug Pagitt. Vote Common Good aimed to help white Evangelical and Catholic Christians stop voting for their own racial and religious advantage and start voting for the common good. I had been involved in electoral politics before, most notably doing some surrogate work for Barack Obama in 2008. But this was a much deeper dive into electoral politics, and I learned a lot.

Early on, I learned this discouraging fact: the vast majority of voters stay loyal to their party and its candidates, year after year, decade after decade. All of the billions of dollars spent on campaign ads and other forms of electioneering only shift a small percentage of swing voters.

That surprised me, because I had a lot of anecdotal evidence of people I knew who had changed, starting with myself. But I realized that my circle of friends and I were outliers. Most people vote as loyal members of their in-group, world without end, amen.

I wondered why so few people change their minds. I started researching the literature on unrationality and bias and eventually wrote an extended essay on the subject, called *Why Don't They Get It? (Overcoming Bias in Others — and Yourself)*, which eventually led to a podcast called *Learning How to See*. That research then led me to study authoritarianism, leading to another extended essay called *The Second Pandemic: Authoritarianism and Your Future*. Through these studies, interactions with others, and personal reflection, I began to better understand why we remain so persistently and deeply divided.

When you study bias, you have to learn about brain science. You discover that our brains are very efficient, meaning that they don't want to waste energy in their quest to keep us alive. And in order to conserve energy, they develop certain shortcuts that happen so fast we aren't even conscious of them. Authoritarian leaders learn how to manipulate us for their advantage by these mental shortcuts.

One of those shortcuts is called confirmation bias. When a new idea comes along that fits in comfortably with what we already think, our brains welcome it. When a new idea comes along that will upset what we already think, our brains get nervous. The brain realizes it would take a lot of energy to rethink our current assumptions. So it gives us a bad feeling about this new idea...before we are even conscious of it, before we even consider whether it might be true.

Another shortcut that our brains employ could be called complementarity bias. If you like me, if you flatter me, if you make me feel good, my brain says, "Ahhhh. I can use some encouragement from a friendly person." So I relax and welcome what you say. But if you challenge me, if you

4

appear angry with me, if you don't seem to agree with me and like me, my brain gets nervous. It says, "This person is going to upset you, and that will take a lot of energy, so I'm just going to give you a bad feeling about them so you won't let yourself be bothered with them."

Let me mention one more, community bias. Our brains know that we depend on our belonging groups for security. So our brains monitor our behavior to be sure that we don't get into too much trouble with our belonging groups. If we were to get kicked out, our lives would grow complicated, which would take a lot of energy and threaten our well-being. So our brains monitor our behavior, including what we say and even what we think, and if we are about to think or say something that would get us in trouble with our belonging group, the brain says, "That's a bad idea. Don't think that. It could get you in trouble." It gives us a bad feeling about that thought so that we will not need to go find a new belonging group.

Put those three biases together — confirmation, complementarity, and community — and then add ten more equally powerful biases, and you can see why we humans tend to flock with birds of a feather who confirm what we already think, who make us feel good about *us* and nervous about *them*, and who value division as a marker of in-group identity. Because of our biases, attempts to bring people over to "our side" often have the opposite effect: hardening both us and them in our postures of mutual hostility, so that eventually, we *humans typically hardly know who we are until we know who we are against.*

Sexism, racism, classism, ableism, regionalism, religious

bigotry, partisanship, and many other -isms flow from this common feature of human thinking.

In large part, that's why we become so persistently polarized, and that's why our divisions can intensify to the point of mutual fear, hatred, and hellish violence.

And that's why this book is so important.

The Apostle Paul once wrote, "If...you bite and devour one another, take care that you are not consumed by one another" (Galatians 5:15 NRSV). In other words, the strategy of identity-by-hostility can easily lead to mutually assured destruction.

In this volume, Brian Allain has brought together a diverse team of creative practitioners of un-division. All of these practitioners are translating peace-making theory into practice on the street, in the neighborhood, and in the human heart. Not only that, but they are developing and revising theory through their practice. That's what makes each contribution so powerful.

In the pages ahead, you'll meet Jeff Burns as he tells the story of how he was transformed from a self-described rabid Islamophobe into a peacemaker, and whose Peace Path crystallizes what he has learned about bridging religious divides. And you'll meet David Bailey, who is helping people get a foretaste in the present of a more peaceful future among races. You'll learn about the Three Practices from Jim Henderson, the Three Shifts from Rabbi Rami Shapiro, and the Six Principles from Todd Deatherage – each chapter a treasure.

Molly La Croix and Parker J. Palmer will help you see how inner work leads to change in the outer world, and the

Rev. Dr. Alexia Salvatierra, Mark Cryderman, and Mark Feldmeir will help you see how faith communities are playing a role in un-dividing America. From Brandan Robertson, you'll learn the value bringing advocacy and activism together to bring change. Amy Julia Becker will help you integrate head, heart, and hands. Each of these contributors bring their diverse experiences to help us create a unified vision of a more peaceful, less divided, less dangerous, more enjoyable world. If you read these chapters with an open mind and heart — and especially if you read them with a group of friends — you will be more equipped than ever to join these practitioners in your own setting, doing your own creative work to help heal our divides.

Environmental genius Annie Leonard famously said, "There is no away. When you throw something away, it must go somewhere." What is true in our physical environment is also true of our social environment. When we identify someone as alien, other, outsider, and enemy, we think we can throw them away. But there is no away; we are neighbors, and we can't escape that fact. Eventually, we will need to learn what Dr. King said: "The only way to get rid of an enemy permanently is to make him your friend."

Brian D. McLaren is an author, speaker, activist, and public theologian. His many books include "Faith After Doubt" and "The Great Spiritual Migration." Learn more about Brian here: brianmclaren.net/

«2»

HEALING DIVIDES
AS CLOWNING

Frank A. Thomas

Healing divides takes a kind of comedy, a kind of laugh-ter, or rather a kind of comedic vision. When I speak of such things, I am not talking about telling jokes or making people laugh exclusively. The comedic vision looks at, what Johan Cilliers and Charles L. Campbell call, the "aesthet-ics of ugliness or repulsion," and yet also carries "a form of beauty."* A comedic vision is to see the beauty in all of the ugliness, and those who recognize the beauty are called "fools," "holy fools" at that. Fools have a wisdom that dis-cerns beauty in all of the ugliness.

In healing divides, there is brute honesty, absurdity, and relentless in facing the downright evil of human existence – our ability to harm, hurt, kill, legislate people out of the human race, and commit the most vicious and heinous acts upon one another. War, violence, poverty, hate, discrimi-nation, rape, murder, molestation, gender violence, abuse, propaganda, human trafficking, addictions, and I could go on. Only a comedic vision can encompass my disappoint-

---

*Charles L. Campbell and Johan H. Cilliers, *Preaching Fools: The Gospel as a Rhetoric of Folly*, (Waco: Baylor University Press, 2012), 6.

8

ment over the absurdity of human violence. In the face of how cruel we are to one another, I have found comfort in a comic vision of life.

In the vein of the ugliness, I live as a minority in a racist society that is often hostile to black presence and black people speaking their truth in its totality. I believe the number one challenge for black people in America is white supremacy. We have dealt with it for generations and will be dealing with it because it is the original and continuing sin of America. James Baldwin said, "To be a Negro in this country and to be relatively conscious is to be in a state of rage almost, almost all of the time — and in one's work."* The comedic vision allows me to be constructive with my rage. My African American foremothers and forefathers did so many constructive and wonderful things with their rage. With a comedic vision, with a constructive rage, they saw beauty in the midst of the ugliness.

A comic vision encompasses tears and laughter as well as humor and lament. The comic vision is expressed in the image of the circus clown. Many clowns have a smile plastered on their faces and some, if one looks carefully, have a tear or tears affixed inexorably to the clown's made up face. The perfect metaphor for healing divides is clowning because the comic vision can handle brute honesty of tears and laughter, the ugliness and beauty of the human experience.

The clown is constantly defeated, tricked, humiliat-

---

* "To be in Rage all the Time," https://www.npr.org/2020/06/01/867153918/-to-be-in-a-rage-almost-all-the-time

ed, and trampled upon. At the circus, the clown does not have the splendor of the trapeze artists, the magicians, and the lion tamers. As Joseph Webb says, these are the folks of "breathtaking human achievements." The clown with a red nose, big sized shoes, and mix-matched clothes, stumbles about and fools around. The clown slips on the banana peel; takes a pie in the face; they throw a ball at the bullseye and the clown drops in the water, taking terrible falls and the like. The clown is vulnerable – slapped, bruised, humiliated, perpetually down, and perpetually assaulted, and it is funny and we all laugh – what a buffoon! What an imbecile!

In the circus, the clown never dies. Harvey Cox puts it this way, the clown is "infinitely vulnerable, but never finally defeated."* No matter how assaulted, the clown never dies. Every now and then the lion will eat the lion tamer and the trapeze artist will fall off the trapeze and die. But the clown lives on. After falling down, the clown always gets back up. The clown always has the last laugh.

The work of healing divides involves the brute honesty, absurdity, and relentless facing of the downright evil of human existence and an unfailing hope that offers the ability to see beauty in the rage of ugliness. The work of healing divides involves slipping on the banana peel, a pie to the face, taking terrible falls, and clowning around.

The clown slips on the banana peel; takes a pie in the face; they throw a ball at the bullseye and the clown drops in the water, taking terrible falls and the like. The clown is

---

*Campbell and Cilliers, 57.

vulnerable, but at the end of the work clowns are left standing, and humanity is much better for it. Campbell and Cilliers say, "clowns transform the circus arena (and for me, life) into a more human, livable space."[*]

Frank A. Thomas is a preacher, teacher, scholar, thinker, lecturer, author, and master coach. His many books include "How to Preach a Dangerous Sermon" and "The Choice." Learn more about Frank here: drfrankathomas.com/

---

[*] Ibid., 159.

Why Heal Our Divides?
We Need to Heal Ourselves

Diana Butler Bass

When first told about this book, *How to Heal Our Divides*, I did not imagine the title as either an invitation or instruction. I thought it was a question: How to heal our divides? How indeed? With social and political division running through everything from the most vexing issues of the day to our own family gatherings, many of us wonder *how* we'll ever get beyond the rifts and ruptures. *How*, when posed as a question, implies a hint of hopeless and surrender. When "how" is more of a directive, it opens up possibilities to learn a new skill or make a change, as in a "how-to" book tinged with optimistic promise. But, if you are like me, my experience of "how-to" books has been marginally successful at best.

There is another question behind the question of how – that is the question of *why*. *Why heal our divides?* After all, human beings have survived despite division for as long as recorded history. Indeed, rulers and politicians are skilled at driving wedges between people around them in order to increase their own power. As Julius Caesar famously remarked *divide et impera*, "divide and conquer."

In our current environment, fear and anger do motivate

communal action, and political expediency often seems the primary goal. One need only be familiar with *The Prince* to know that modern politics follows the lead of Niccolo Machiavelli far more than the social vision of any ethical or religious master – Moses, the Buddha, and Jesus included.

And so, we find ourselves in a world echoing Gordon Gecko's famous 1980s dictum, "greed is good," where the contemporary American political creed seems to be "division is gain."

Of course, most of the readers of this book will not agree with Julius Caesar, Machiavelli, or Gordon Gecko. We believe such an approach to community is wrong, immoral, violent, and, ultimately, destructive. Like Cardinal Pole who read *The Prince* upon its publication, and remarked: "I found this type of book to be written by an enemy of the human race. It explains every means whereby religion, justice and any inclination toward virtue could be destroyed." In 1559, the Catholic Church placed Machiavelli's work on its index of forbidden books – a move (of course) that only made his ideas more popular. Fostering animus between people for the sake of political gain is *not* a moral good. Religions emphasize peace and unity, and they offer ethical visions for a world of equanimity and justice. Even when church authorities engaged in division, they mouthed disdain for it – unable to stamp such an unscrupulous approach with their approval.

Division is one of the most persistent political strategies in the western world. You might say it is our practice, the most deeply ingrained of our political habits. It certainly isn't new. *Why heal our divides?* The question might be answered: You can't. History teaches us that Machiavelli will always be with us – and will most often win.

Why even try to heal our divides?

Because it matters. For our communities, our neighbors. Of course. But it also matters for our own lives.

In 1892, William James wrote, "All our life, so far as it has definite form, is but a mass of habits." A large body of research since then has confirmed how our lives are composed of routinized practices, the habits we develop over years. One recent study found that 40 percent of the participants' daily actions did not come from intentional choice, but were things they did from habit.

America is a culture that aspires to unity – *e pluribus unum* – but has habituated division. Blame it on Caesar, Machiavelli, Gordon Gecko or whomever. Truth is, we've a national habit of finger pointing, blaming others, assigning people to categories, and pressing advantage for our own side. We've a divided national soul, and that line of division runs right through each of our own hearts. Even when we say we want to get beyond division and invective, many (including me) secretly think, "But I don't want to be with *those* people. They are beyond the pale. You can't make peace with *them*."

When I finally admit that division isn't just external but a way of thinking and acting that I've learned, it hurts. I may preach a good sermon on nonviolence or taking down the walls of hostility between people, but deep inside, I'm uneasily grateful that something still separates me from others. The boundary between my moral rightness and another's ethical failing seems necessary to protect. Those boundaries become hidden prejudices, the prejudices turn into partisanship, and all-too-often, partisanship crystallizes as bigotry. For good people, this internal process can be subtle, deniable, and shameful. But it is part of our habituation into being American – a people who proclaim unity while building walls that divide.

Why heal our divides? Because if we do, we heal ourselves.

New Testament scholar Stephen Patterson has recently argued that the first Christian creed was not a proclamation of separation from others (believers from nonbelievers); rather it was a declaration of human solidarity. That creed was part of the very first baptismal liturgies of those who followed Jesus:

For you are all children of God in the Spirit.

There is no Jew or Greek;

There is no slave or free;

There is no male and female.

For you are all one in the Spirit.

He insists that Christianity was successful because it imparted a social vision of unity in a deeply divided world and called people to a new identity: "We human beings are naturally clannish and partisan: we are defined by who we are not. We are not *them*. This creed claims that there is no us, no them. We are all one. We are all children of God." (Patterson, *The Forgotten Creed*, p. 5)

Not only did the first Christians proclaim these words, they practiced them in their communities. They developed habits of including others, of breaking down barriers, of eating with and befriending those whom they once found objectionable. They literally showed Roman society that it

15

was possible – and desirable – to love every neighbor without regard to religion, class, or gender. For at least some time in the early years of Christianity's existence, the faith was marked by its insistence of the common kinship of humankind – that we could, indeed, be one. And there is evidence that they practiced what they preached.

And so this volume. Is the American creed possible? That *e pluribus unum* we recite? Or are we forever consigned to the historical habits that confirm the we and demonize *them*? History reminds us that such creeds must be embodied in communities of practice, where we are called into a vision of human solidarity, where we make new habits together, where we establish peace across the most durable barriers, and where we get in trouble for standing as one against the political expediency of division.

When I commit myself to that creed, when I find myself in such a community, the divide in my own heart lessens. Something within heals. Creed and community remind me that changing habits is hard, and practicing solidarity involves wrestling with my own failures. But, with the help of others, each one of us can mend the fault lines in our own lives and lend our hands to repair the world.

Read these essays and discover you are not alone. You have friends, co-workers, mentors, and guides for the way.

Diana Butler Bass is an award-winning author, popular speaker, inspiring preacher, and one of America's most trusted commentators on religion and contemporary spirituality. Her many books include "Freeing Jesus" and "Grateful." Learn more about Diana here: dianabutlerbass.com/

"Nothing New Under the Sun": Opposing Racism Today

Michael W. Waters

A round midnight on October 16, 1915, William Joseph Simmons, a Methodist minister, ascended Stone Mountain in Georgia with fifteen men. He built an altar to his god and laid upon it a Bible, a sword, and an American flag. A cross was also set ablaze. Hence, the second rise of the Ku Klux Klan was born.

Later, reflecting on that day, Simmons declared, "The angels that have anxiously watched the reformation from its beginnings must have hovered about Stone Mountain and shouted hosannas to the highest heavens." During Simmons's seven years of leadership, the Klan experienced dramatic growth. Facilitating acts of racial terrorism across America, the Klan gained majority control over several statehouses and made public witness of their increasing influence by marching through the streets of Washington, D.C.

The racial hatred currently being spawned across America is not new. This is not the first time that the god of white supremacy has been worshipped in both citadels of power and churches. Yet, this does not diminish the clear and present danger that it poses. White supremacy comes with a body count, and when racism reigns, death runs rampant, too.

The courageous work of antiracists engaged in the ongoing struggle for racial liberation saves lives. Literally. The work of the diverse organizations highlighted in this volume, and many others who are not, is vitally important.

The divides in America are readily apparent. Yet, the roots of these divides are not as distinguishable for many. Before we can heal these divides, we must take full inventory of the roots from which they spring. Oftentimes, our divides result from a form of idol worship. When our god is a manifestation of our unsubstantiated fears and greed, we follow a god shaped and formed exclusively to serve our own callous interests, as opposed to the God who shapes and forms us as a reflection of Godself to care for the concerns of others.

The author of Ecclesiastes opined, "History merely repeats itself. It has all been done before. Nothing under the sun is truly new" (1:9 NLT). Racism and racial oppression are not new, but just as they are not new, neither is our opposition to them. This truth is a well of hope. We have been gifted with a blueprint for transformative struggle. In multiple generations before us we find persons who combated these evils with courage and consistency, persons brave enough to bend the arc towards justice knowing that it does not bend itself, persons who bear witness to the light of God in the whole of humanity and who work boldly against any force seeking to diminish that light.

Coretta Scott King said, "Struggle is a never-ending process. Freedom is never really won; you earn it and win it in every generation." As in generations past, we must boldly, courageously, and consistently pick up the mantle of justice and advance the cause of freedom forward against this familiar foe.

With faith in God and in community with each other, we will certainly prevail.

Michael W. Waters is an award-winning author, professor, activist, social commentator, and the founder and Lead Pastor of Abundant Life A.M.E. Church in Dallas, Texas. Learn more about Michael: michaelwwaters.com/

PART TWO

WAYS YOU CAN GET INVOLVED

«5»

LIVING INTO GOD'S DREAM

Dismantling Racism in Atlanta and Beyond

Catherine Meeks

Many years ago the Episcopal General Convention mandated that all leaders in the church had to participate in anti-racism training and that commissions should be organized to make sure that the mandate was met. The Diocese of Atlanta took the resolution seriously and organized an Anti-racism Commission and charged it with the task of getting folks trained.

But, the commission did not find it easy to facilitate its work because folks who were mandated to participate in the training resented that fact and many people became quite proficient at finding ways to avoid it. An unfortunate spirit of negativity began to form around the Anti-racism Commission in general and the workshop sessions in particular. The background regarding our journey from Commission to Center is integral to understanding the organic nature of the racial healing work that the Center engages and shares locally, regionally, nationally and internationally.

At the point that there were the most complaints about the racial healing work in the Diocese, I was invited to become the chair of the commission. This invitation came after the training workshops had been dormant for about six months and there was a significant backlog of folks who were to be ordained or assume other leadership positions and could not go forward because the required workshop was not available.

As soon as I became the chair, we began a conversation about changing the name of the group to Beloved Community: Commission for Dismantling Racism instead of the Anti-racism Commission. The name change was significant because it embodied the mission of the group which was designed to work toward establishing beloved community, and, in order to do that, we needed to dismantle racism. Thus the name change helped to generate a more positive spirit around the work, and we moved on to the task of changing the structure of the dismantling racism workshop.

The previous structure was quite reliant on a rather corporate model without any particular emphasis upon spirituality or any theological framework. The re-imagining process led to creating a new format that made the Eucharist a part of the training day with a very intentional focus upon dismantling racism work as spiritual formation. Prior to this re-imagining process, it was very easy to see the day's workshop more as a chore that had to be completed in order to serve in a particular capacity rather than seeing it as being a part of one's ongoing spiritual formation. Dismantling racism work is not a box to check off after completing a one day workshop; it is a lifetime of inner and outer work that will last throughout a person's entire life. It is long-term, and it requires an entire lifetime of commit-ment to the work, in the same manner that other parts of the spiritual journey is engaged. No one who participates in parish or congregational membership has been invited to quit paying their pledge or attending services simply because they have been faithful for ten, fifteen or twenty years. The same is true with dismantling racism work: it must continue for the duration of one's life.

The creation of a curriculum, which is grounded in the Eucharist and emphasizes dismantling racism as part of spiritual formation, invigorated our work beyond anything we could have imagined. The curriculum is built on the premise that such formation is necessary for anyone who hopes to become a spiritually mature person. Prior to the complete discontinuance of the workshops there had been two or three a year offered. When we got to our fourth year with the new format and focus, we were hosting eight to twelve workshops with at least twenty participants in each class. The new energy and enthusiasm regarding the work-shops can mostly be attributed to the addition of the Eucha-rist and the focus upon overall lifetime spiritual formation as the primary foundation for the work. The news about the newly formatted workshops and other work that grew out of those workshops spread around the wider church. Parishioners from several other dioceses inquired about participating in our training sessions. We were delighted to welcome guests from the wider church, but as the message became more widespread the demand continued to grow beyond our capacity to meet it.

Thus, Bishop Robert C. Wright realized that we had

outgrown ourselves as a commission and that we needed to consider a next step for ourselves. This realization
came at the conclusion of seven years of diligent work by
the Beloved Community Commission using the Eucharist
Centered Dismantling Racism curriculum. After extensive
conversations with Presiding Bishop Michael B. Curry and
others who shared the vision, we arrived at the decision to
open the Absalom Jones Episcopal Center for Racial Healing which embodies all of the work that the Commission
was charged to do plus any and all new ways to work for
racial healing.

Bishop Curry was primarily concerned about establishing an entity that could assist dioceses and parishes in
getting their work to go beyond simply having a handful
of workshops on dismantling racism and then considering the work to be complete. Before the Commission was
retired, we had demonstrated quite clearly that there was
much work to do beyond the training day. We had hosted
pilgrimages and book studies, developed a youth curriculum for sixth to twelfth grade, screened films, hosted conversations on race, and organized a three-year campaign
to remember the lynched in our state. This energetic approach to the work as a commission helped to propel the
process of founding the Center.

In early October 2017, the Center for Racial Healing
hosted its official opening with more than two hundred
guests from across the United States and West Africa
crowded into our small chapel (a chapel that is designed to
comfortably seat about 125 people). It was a glorious day
and one of the most exciting moments for all of us who

had worked tirelessly for eight years laying the foundation that the Center now enjoys. It is easy for it to appear that the Center popped up much like mushrooms that spontaneously pop up after summer rains appear to do, but it is important to remember that the work grew in an organic and clear manner from one level to another. The good news is that the Center has continued to follow patterns that are infused with energy from the beginning. Therefore, we do not have to make heroic efforts to infuse energy into projects that can be reluctant about thriving.

The Center will be four years old in October of 2021. It has grown from a small entity with one full-time staff person and a part-time intern to a staff of three full-time persons and one half-time contractor. The work was heavily focused in the Diocese of Atlanta initially and that work has spread throughout sixty-five of the ninety-nine dioceses in the Episcopal Church, including Latin America. The work has been done in many dioceses who have called upon us for coaching, counsel, conversation partnership and general support. The Center continues to be encouraged to stay focused and to stay grounded in the theological and spiritual root systems that inform us about the ways in which we must continue to embrace dismantling racism and any other types of oppression that seek to hinder God's people's quest for freedom.

The Center is beginning to work on designing a racial healing curriculum for K-5 grades which will expand our courses of study for K-adulthood regarding dismantling racism. The current curriculum for sixth through twelfth graders is available through Church Publishing after the completion of the prerequisites for its use. It has become quite popular and is being used across the wider church. Along with widespread use of the youth curriculum is continued growth of interest in the workshop for adults. We are currently presenting twenty-five adult classes per year and we have designed an apprenticeship model for assisting dioceses across the wider church in identifying and training a group of facilitators in their respective locations so they can be more self-sufficient in getting this initial part of their work done. While the Center is happy to witness the level of interest that is being generated around the country regarding stepping up to the racial healing challenge and to help when we can, we are not equipped to offer training to all who will need it. We prefer to assist groups in becoming competent themselves instead of having to rely on the Center or any other entity. Also,this model serves the larger purpose of allowing the Center to be an encourager to the groups who engage with it to go deeper into the racial healing work.

The Center for Racial Healing is located across the street from the historic Atlanta University Consortium which consists of Morehouse, Spelman, Morris Brown, Interdenominational Theological Center (formerly Clark College), and Atlanta University who have merged to become Clark Atlanta-University. It is situated quite strategically with its front facing the campuses and its back facing a community that is suffering economic and spiritual blight. This location offers the Center an opportunity to work with the members of the local community, the campus community, its Episcopal constituency at the local level, all the while reaching across the United States to the wider church as well as internationally. Though this is challenging, it is a blessing for the Center to have such an opportunity to expand its reach and explore multiple layers of partnerships with a diverse group of partners. Thus far the desire to collaborate has led the Center to partner with local parishes, selected members of the medical community in regards to the Covid-19 crisis, local educational leaders in the K-12 arena, and local citizens who helped the Center to keep an intergenerational focus to its work.

The Center is continuing to engage with seminaries to encourage them in expanding their racial healing and justice training for their students; promoting justice pilgrimages for clergy across the wider church (which requires a six-month commitment of intentional racial healing work from them); reimagining policing and public safety; providing educational opportunities; and advocating in regards to health inequity, mass incarceration, immigration, and environmental justice. Much of this work will be done under the umbrella of the Bishop Barbara Harris Justice Project which was named to honor her in 2019 and supports the outreach and advocacy initiatives of the Center.

Catherine Meeks, Ph.D. serves as Executive Director of the Absalom Jones Center for Racial Healing; she is Former Chair of the Beloved Community: Commission for Dismantling Racism.

Learn more about Catherine: centerforracialhealing.org/about

Learn more about The Absalom Jones Center for Racial Healing: howtohealourdivides.com/absalom-jones-center-for-racial-healing/

HEALING OUR DIVIDES

Preaching the Common Good

Mark Feldmeir

Christians will go to extraordinary lengths to avoid mixing politics and church. Some have even said that mixing church and politics is like mixing ice cream and manure. It doesn't do much for the manure, but it sure does ruin the ice cream.

In 2019, I set out to disprove the notion that there is no place in the pulpit for politics. My ultimate aim was to demonstrate that Hebrew and Christian Scriptures are not politically neutral, and that when Christians are in church, they should actually be at their most political.

By political I do not mean partisan. The word "politics" comes from the Greek "polis," meaning "affairs of the cities." To do politics is to be concerned about the affairs of the communities in which we live; to do politics in church is to ask, "What does the gospel of Jesus Christ say about how I should live in my community and what my responsibility should be to the people who are members of that community?"

This is a politics of compassion, and it is vastly different from the politics of contempt that has swept across America's political landscape in recent years. A politics of compassion transcends "issue politics" and "culture wars" and calls us to consider what kind of communities we want to live in, what kind of neighbors we want to be, and how we might collectively order our lives to work together for the common good.

While a politics of compassion is not exclusive to the teachings of Jesus of Nazareth and can be found in all three Abrahamic traditions, Jesus seemed to embody it most fully in his life and teaching ministry. He captured it most compellingly in his Parable of the Last Judgment, which asks of us: "When I was hungry, thirsty, sick and in prison, did you care? When I was your neighbor in disguise, your fellow citizen, a stranger, did you love me?" (Matthew 25).

This is the only kind of politics that mattered to Jesus, and it's the one kind of politics that can inspire people of faith from both sides of the political aisle to find enough common ground to work together for the common good.

In 2019, I led the people of St. Andrew United Methodist Church, where I serve as Sr. Pastor, through an 8-part sermon series in which we explored some of the most contentious political issues of our day: climate change, immigration, racism, health care, medical aid in dying, LGBTQ inclusion, Islamic extremism, and suicide. We addressed these issues through the lens of Scripture, reason, our faith experience, and centuries of Christian tradition. Over those 8 weeks, weekly worship attendance at St. Andrew increased by an average of 18%. Countless members of St. Andrew invited their neighbors and colleagues to church for the first time. Dozens from the Denver Metro who had no previous relationship with St. Andrew attended each week; many later joined the membership of St. Andrew.

Why did this series resonate so clearly with people of diverse political perspectives? How did we address such divisive issues in church without alienating some of our people? What did we learn together that might inform how we negotiate political conversations with those with whom we disagree? I offer three takeaways:

First, we can't heal the divides unless we honestly and fairly name the issues that divide us, identify the specific points of fissure on those issues, and claim the common ground upon which we can work together for the common good.

Setting aside the soundbites and talking points that dominate our newsfeeds, we asked: how does scripture, along with our tradition, reason, and experience, speak to this issue? How have we, as a nation, addressed this issue in the past? What mistakes did we make, and what lessons have we learned from our history? On each of these particular issues, what specifically do people today tend most to disagree about?

Naming and re-framing the issues in this fashion allowed us to establish common ground by proposing "axioms" that helped us think more reasonably about the issues. An axiom is a statement that is taken to be self-evidently true, in order to serve as a premise or starting point for further reasoning. In classic philosophy, an axiom is an assertion so well established that it's accepted without controversy or question. Some examples include: the sun rises from the east; humans have one brain; two parallel lines never bisect each other.

Consider the following axioms:

On the issue of Islamic extremism: "Violence is neither a normative behavior nor a core tenant of Islam."

On the issue of racism in America: "Race is the child of racism, not the father."

On the issue of immigration: "We are all originally from somewhere else."

Such practical and common-sense axioms, along with dozens of others, served as stepping stones that progressively led people to find common ground, mutuality, and shared solutions.

Second, we can only heal our divides by physically bringing people together in safe, highly structured dialogue groups, to better and more honestly understand the experiences, feelings, and beliefs of those on the other side, and to be better understood by others. The objective in doing so is to help people feel less hostile and less estranged toward those on the other side, and to feel better equipped to start constructive conversations grounded in compassion and generosity of spirit.

Each week throughout the series, several groups of 12 people gathered to engage in conversation and deep listening. A resource was provided that included a guiding prayer and centering exercise, a scripture reading related to the specific issue, some basic ground rules for listening and sharing, and several questions focused on one's personal experience.

Consider, for example, the following questions:

On the issue of racism: "How well informed are you about the history of racism in your own city or communi-

33

ty? What can you share about this history that others may not know?"

On the issue of immigration: "What brought your ancestors to the U.S.? What was their country of origin? When did they arrive and where did they settle?"

On the issue of Islamic extremism: "Do you personally have any friends, colleagues, or neighbors who are Muslim? If so, what is important to them? What has been the nature of your interactions or relationships with them?"

Such questions address one significant underlying reason we tend to become so polarized—namely, our personal and collective trauma and grievances that associate with a profound sense of insignificance and an existential fear that we, or our "tribe," are becoming increasingly more neglected, marginalized, and forgotten.

Third, we can only heal our divides by acknowledging that the vast majority of Americans are not nearly as polarized in their actual convictions as the current political rhetoric suggests. National polling reveals over and over again that there is actually broad agreement on most of the controversial issues of our day. We have far more in common than we've been led to believe by the media, which are driven by profit, and our political institutions, which are motivated by power. Each are highly organized and resourced to amplify and exploit the differences among us. Each preach a message that elevates proximate things over ultimate things. Each thrive on, and perpetuate, a kind of binary thinking that compels us—even coerces us—to view our neighbors in terms good and evil, right and wrong, friend and enemy. The result is that we have never felt more isolated, socially disconnected, and lonely as individuals.

Throughout the sermon series, members were invited, in advance of the sermon, to participate in a weekly survey about their attitudes and beliefs regarding the issue to be addressed. The surveys consisted of 5 to 8 questions, based loosely on questions from national polls on the same issues. On average, 700 respondents, representing diverse political perspectives and affiliations, participated each week. In each of the 8 surveys, 80-90% of respondents expressed views that reflected a generally moderate perspective; less than 10% expressed views that would be considered "extreme left" or "extreme right." The aggregate responses to the survey were projected on a screen in real-time during the delivery of the sermon as a way to suggest that, despite our diverse political perspectives, we have far more in common than we might believe.

Some of what deeply and intractably divides us is a matter of perception. The majority of Americans are not on the extremes of any of these issues, but most of what we hear and read is from people who reflect more extreme views. Our natural tendency is to conceptualize everyone on the other side of the political spectrum as though they are representative of the leaders and proponents of that side. Correcting this misperception is key to recognizing that we share ultimate goals that need to be achieved for the sake of the common good—goals that both sides desire, but neither side can achieve without the cooperation of the other side.

The divides in our nation, in our neighborhoods, even in our families, are real. But they do not have to be eternal or all-consuming. By naming and reframing the issues, bringing people together for honest and fair conversations, and affirming that we have more in common than we are led to believe, we can find enough common ground to heal the divides and work together for the common good.

Mark Feldmeir is the author of four books, including his latest work, "A House Divided: Engaging the Issues through a Politics of Compassion." Learn more about Mark Feldmeir: markfeldmeir.com

Learn more about St. Andrew United Methodist Church: gostandrew.com

‹‹7›› THE FUTURE OF CHURCH

*Training a New Generation
of Leaders Seeking to Bridge the
Divide Between Good Intentions
and Lasting Social Impact*

Rich Tafel

Now is the time for the Christian Church in America to become the place where young leaders can develop their inner spiritual life and the skills to transform society for the better.

We live in a time of deep division with seemingly unsolvable challenges. We lack leaders who have both a deep spiritual life and also know how to launch a social business or change public policy. To meet this challenge, churches must rise up to provide the space, training, and resources for a rising generation of spiritual entrepreneurs.

Spiritual entrepreneurs integrate their mystical life with the practical skills to transform unjust systems. In my own life, I translate across sectors serving as the Director of Raffa Social Capital Advisors where I work with investors and social ventures seeking to create businesses for good. In addition, I serve as the co-founder of the American Project at Pepperdine School of Public Policy where we seek to find common ground between left and right. This all gets integrated in my pastoral work at Church of the Holy City where we are creating an incubator for spiritual entrepreneur leaders.

I've spent the past twenty years as a strategist in the social entrepreneur movement, the ten years before that as a political player, and the five years before that working at a church. What I've learned is that the problems facing our world require leaders grounded in deep faith in God and well versed in the skills of business and politics. I call these leaders spiritual entrepreneurs.

They seek to create businesses, churches, and political movements to create a better world. But spiritual entrepreneurs are explicit in their work that they are motivated, inspired, and sustained through the power of God. In 2006, I launched my first spiritual entrepreneur leadership coaching program, which was subscribed almost entirely by ordained ministers who were taught nothing about how to launch a business or organization. What became clear was these ministers were given no training in running business, governance or policy change. They were being set up for failure.

Spiritual entrepreneurs integrate the power of God to the action necessary to bring heaven to earth. Yet, social change leaders inspired by their spiritual life must piece together their own training to have an impact. When I graduated from Harvard Divinity School I was knowledgeable about systematic theology yet ignorant of how practically to change systems. Spiritual entrepreneurs can bridge this divide, and churches can become the incubators of a rising generation.

Today, six thousand churches are closing each year in America. Young people no longer view church as a place to gain this training. This is the moment that the church must reimagine its role to be the space that bridges the greatest divide between our souls and our work.

How can this be done?

Let me share practical lessons in my own practice and the work we've been experimenting with at my church.

In 2016, I took on the pastorate of Church of the Holy City in Washington DC, the national church of the Swedenborgian Church. The church, built in 1896, holds three hundred people. It was down to only five members over seventy years old. The building itself faced two million dollars in needed maintenance (made clear by the wooden electrical circuit box). The denomination and the remaining members had one last shot at saving the space.

What looked like a crisis was an opportunity to turn this lovely church into a spiritual entrepreneur incubator. While this strategy will be different for each church, I'll share three major steps you could take with your church to create your own spiritual entrepreneur incubator.

1. Get Your House of Worship in Order: Make Your Church a Start Up Hub

You cannot be a spiritual enterprise incubator until you imagine your church like a business. With little or no revenue and no marketing, yet intense maintenance needs, we first needed to get our house of worship in order. The first step is to transform the church building from a liability to an asset. Some churches are too far gone to be able to be renovated. I've advised churches in this situation how to sell the asset and create a trust to invest in new opportunities. I'll focus here on transforming the building.

The gorgeous church building on 16th Street had sought to be of service to local meditation, yoga, and karate groups. It opened its doors for free for musical events. The once booming wedding business had declined.

The challenge was that an under-capitalized building made rentals difficult. One extra light plugged in would shut the system down. Water leaking undermined events and destroyed entire rooms. Our events were plagued by freezing in winter and brutal baked heat in summer.

Each church has its own challenges. But if we can flip the mindset that this is an asset, not a liability, we can transform it in real life. Funding for church renovation has got to become much more creative with a pitch that inspires funders. In our case the church is owned by the denomination who partnered with us on repairs. As the vision and progress grew we were able to obtain outside grants for historic repair.

This is critical for momentum. One week after securing one large loan to do repairs, the ceiling in the basement collapsed from water damage. Thank God no one was there that night. Had that roof collapsed and I didn't have a financial plan, I would have no choice but to sell the building with the damage. I count it as an act of divine providence that funds came before the crash.

Churches need to seek the expertise of those who understand real estate and train pastors with the basic knowledge of building management.

As the building is being repaired it must be strategically used for rental purposes. Churches are safe renting to other spiritual communities, but if the rentals are outside of the church mission they can be taxed. This fear of being taxed as a nonprofit leads most churches to stop there, but with proper accounting this can be done.

An important step was hiring a leader who has the social skills to engage the community. Shalonda Ingram had attended one of our spiritual entrepreneur discussions. Her expertise was events. Her diversity business, Born Brown, meant she had a built-in network of community leaders. As a Black woman she was well aware that our city was deeply racially segregated and our church was not even known within the surrounding community, particularly the Black community.

We created a fee structure based on a base fee and revenues from rentals. She further developed a model, much like Airbnb, called Peer Space, to rent our spaces out to groups aligned to our mission. Just as repairs were in good enough shape to really rent we were hit by the pandemic. Through her entrepreneurial spirit, she pivoted to renting the space to record speeches, sermons, and documentaries. Had we not invested in this building maintenance work before the pandemic we likely would have not survived financially.

Churches must first get their house in order before they can be useful training center to the rising generation.

2. Develop Young Leaders' Inner Life

All active churches have a weekly Sunday service of some kind. Instead of completely reinventing the wheel, transform Sunday services into a relevant space for people to learn, question, discuss, and grow their spiritual life in a humble and interactive way.

Young people in our community might be intrigued by our use of the word "entrepreneur," but in our city that wasn't enough. In my surveys and focus groups of young socially responsible leaders, they repeatedly told me that the biggest barrier to their being involved with "church" was the word "church." Church for them meant homophobia, sexism, and racism. It meant exclusion of other faiths. To a generation whose highest values are inclusion and justice, church wasn't just a passive player in the culture. It was the enemy.

To address this challenge, we worked to make it very clear our church was a sanctuary for all voices.

We've also used our worship time to introduce difficult topics, such as, racism, trans issues, homophobia, and polarized politics. Often we use a dialogue sermon to share different viewpoints, or I ask experts to join me during the social dialogue. Other times I interview experts. Our message is we don't need to agree but we do need to respect.

Churches must hold the space for differing viewpoints where young leaders can deepen their inner life. As an urban church, our congregation is largely progressive, particularly the younger members. The political polarization has been an even greater issue of division than other issues. It's the one issue members get nervous speaking about the most. Our culture doesn't teach us how to hold political discussion, but our church, where everyone is heard, is changing that.

I have tried to make the sermon messages both thoughtful and also practical, using what I'd learned in my life coaching practice. I began asking if anyone had a question. First, afraid to speak, we began a facilitated discussion. The feedback, questions, and insights from others transformed learning from "a pastor with all the answers" to a chance for people to gain their voice and ask their questions. My experience in facilitations became critical to allow a safe space to ask questions. Soon it was the most popular part of the service. In respect for time, I moved it to after the formal benediction. I began inviting experts on topics generated by the group who co-lead the discussion.

The word "church" was one of the biggest barriers to entry. So we began a series of dinners and discussions reaching out to existing social entrepreneur networks to discuss spiritual topics. Simply getting participants into the church to experience inclusion can be healing and can build your incubator brand.

3. Impact Life Training:
Provide Coaching, Training, and Resources;
Create Cohorts Monday through Saturday

Young leaders who live in the community outside the church will warm up to the idea of renting church space long before they trust it is a space they can learn about their soul or business life. Consider offering entrepreneurs the chance to rent a desk providing much needed space. Coming to church might be the last part of their engagement, but providing courses and teaching in morality, purpose, and life management will help meet their needs.

A Mastermind group is also a great place to start for church. Have participants come, and each week feature one who needs help from others. Prepare a rough outline but roll with the evolution of the model. As the topic moves to changing political systems, bring in experts who have changed policies. When the issue is generating revenue or marketing, reach out to spirit-inspired experts to share what they've learned. Have the church pick up the tab for food and space rental and you'll be amazed.

We are just now launching our second spiritual entrepreneur cohort. Four themes will be taught in eight classes with one week focused on the inner and the next the impact business they are creating. True to the new way of operating in the world, the model will be co-created with participants with me as facilitator. What you plan in a curriculum like this will not be what you do. Pay attention to the group and the voice of the Holy Spirit as this unfolds.

While I am still pulling teeth to have young people come to church, there's a waiting list of young leaders who want coaching, training, and space to launch their ventures. We are now looking to put our classes online for other groups interested in using this model.

The strategy of our church is integration. Churches that welcome the rising generation of leaders by helping them create their social enterprise and offering them access to the transforming wisdom of faith will become sought after training locations who provide the strategies required to transform the world for good.

How to Start

Examine the three major areas I've outlined here. Make clear the trainers and experts you'll need to get this work done. There are facilitators, business experts, lobbyists, accountants, and lawyers out there who can help you. Put together the team, get the word out, and the young leaders may begin to express interest. The brand of church is a tough one to overcome, but by showing you are a spiritual entrepreneur incubator you might find surprising interest.

There's never been a more critical time for churches to become the space to train a rising generation on the way to develop a profound spiritual life with the practical skills to bring heaven to earth.

Rev. Rich Tafel serves as a pastor, social venture strategist and facilitator of political dialogue. Learn more about Rich:
linkedin.com/in/richtafel

Learn more about Church of the Holy City: holycitydc.org/

United in Joint Mission

The Power of Right Relationship to Heal the Divides

Rev. Dr. Alexia Salvatierra

The Chair of the Board of the 18,000 member, mostly white Republican, megachurch in Southern California had been participating for several months in a prison visitation ministry. Unlike most prison ministries, this particular ministry was with children and youth in an immigrant detention facility. The chair had been part of a ministry team including volunteers from a primarily Hispanic immigrant megachurch in a neighboring city. In the training for the program, he had learned about Biblical perspectives on immigration as well as the history and current legal realities of the immigration system.

Then came the day that he and his teammate, a leader on the Church Council of the Hispanic congregation, arrived at the facility and encountered a young man who had accepted Christ in the program. He was crying, terrified. He had learned that he was scheduled to be deported, sure that he was targeted for assassination by predatory organized crime syndicates in his home country. The Chair of the Board turned to his ministry partner in outrage. "What is going on here?" he said. "What can we do to stop this?". His teammate responded, "My cousin was deported a month ago. He was killed on arrival." The Chair of the Board went right to the desk of the Senior Pastor. He said "The Board has to study this issue. We have a crisis going on in our community and we need to understand it better."

The Senior Pastor was nervous, but the Chair was a major donor as well as leader. The Board studied a book by Matt Soerens and Jenny Yang of World Relief, the humanitarian organization of the National Association of Evangelicals. Their study also included presentations by volunteers in the program, who shared their lived experience. The church became a major leader in a new Welcoming the Stranger network. When they went to visit their notoriously anti-immigrant Congressional representative (whom many of them had helped elect), he had assumed they would want more restrictive immigration policies and had prepared for the meeting accordingly. He was in shock when he heard not only their position, but also the mutual trust and tangible unity between their church leaders and the Hispanic immigrant church leaders.

This story is a snapshot of an alternative approach to healing the divides, an approach rooted in changing hearts before changing minds, standing together on the common sacred ground of our faith. In Southern California, we have been bringing people together across the divide on the sacred ground of common faith and shared experience of joint mission since 2006. Since December of 2016, the primary vehicle and context for this work is *Matthew 25/ Mateo 25*, an intentional bipartisan network of immigrant and non-immigrant Christians, primarily evangelical, who come together to stand with and defend vulnerable individuals and families in the name and Spirit of Jesus.

Matthew 25/Mateo 25 formed as a response to the election of Donald Trump as President. A number of Christian leaders, including prominent evangelical leaders, knew that the new administration might be bad news for immigrants. We were worried. We called ourselves Matthew 25 after the statement by Jesus in Matthew 25:35 that our welcome or rejection of the stranger was a welcome or rejection of Him. We did not all share the same opinions about policy nor did we identify with the same political party, but we all knew people who were vulnerable to family separation and/or deportation if policies became more restrictive. More importantly, we knew these vulnerable families as brothers and sisters, people whom we trusted.

Many of us also knew that the church had a unique potential role to play in resolving the immigration crisis in the U.S. The vast majority of Americans know that the immigration system is ineffective. Those who have had direct experience with the system, or know someone who has, realize that it is also illogical and inhumane. We have had two thoroughly bipartisan federal immigration reform proposals (in 2007 and 2013). The policy components of these proposals polled at over 70%. Most Americans want an immigration system that is effective, logical, and humane. However, not only have we been unable to pass either of these proposals, we have not passed any version of the Dream Act (which polls at 90%). The Dream Act would create a path to legal residency for people who were brought to this country as children and who meet a set of conditions. We have not been able to pass this legislation because the average American does not see immigration as a priority; it does not affect them directly. They do not contact their representatives about their desire for a better system. Your average American lacks any passion for the issue. Immigrant networks do not lack passion, but they lack hope. They know that they are in the minority.

Followers of Jesus are mandated to care passionately about all people, not just ourselves and our loved ones, and we are called to act on hope, even in apparently hopeless situations. The church, a community where immigrants and non-immigrants come together, could be the place where passion and hope are exchanged – where non-immigrants become passionate because they know and trust those who are most affected, and where immigrants become hopeful because they know people who will join and help them. However, that does not happen unless immigrant and non-immigrant Christians come together spiritually, as trusted equals, as family. The deepest connections, we have found, happen in the trenches. When people act out their faith together in love, they forge a bond between them that allows for hard conversations to occur naturally.

In *Matthew 25/Mateo 25*, we come together around specific families who are facing potential deportation – including asylum seekers. (We are the lead agency for the Ecumenical Collaboration for Asylum Seekers, an ecumenical multi-denominational coalition.) Christians have been forming support circles for refugees since WWII. The difference in these circles is that immigrants and non-immigrants work together as equals in supporting the families – and the families are also networked to support each other. Charity, in which one group is helping another, does not produce the kind of trust, respect and intimacy that arises in peer relationships in which both groups are working together to help those in need.

There are two aspects of *Matthew 25/Mateo 25*'s work that are essential to our success. In addition to immigrant and non-immigrant Christians, the third arm of *M25* is our Puente (bridge) network – bilingual, bicultural Latinx Millennials who serve as a bridge between immigrant and non-immigrant communities. In our context, their identity becomes vocation as they enable the two groups to communicate and work together well. As part of their duties, our Puente network leads cross-border immersion experiences, connecting immigrant realities in the United States with root causes. On our last trip, a white evangelical leader from the Midwest said that we had changed her life that day, because we had "changed the hero." The 20 year old Puente standing next to her said "I never thought of myself as a hero before." Instead of the hero being the white citizens who help, in *M25*, the guests themselves and the immigrant and Puente volunteers who support them become the heroes. In the process, we see a new kind of relationship and a new level of unity develop across the lines of immigration status and political affiliation. In this kind of relationship, hearts are changed, then minds are changed, and the exchange of passion and hope fuels effective advocacy.

M25 also collaborates with the Centro Latino of Fuller Theological Seminary and Sojourners to run an online

professional certificate program that equips pastoral leaders, Spanish-speaking and Puentes, to engage their congregations in responding to the immigration crisis. When two
groups with different levels of societal power try to work
together, the group with more power and resources tends
to dominate and the opportunity for peer intimacy is lost.
It really helps to provide another level of training to those
with less power. When a border-based legal firm helped
the parents who had been separated from their children
in the Spring of 2017 to return for reunification, one of
the graduates of the *M25* certificate program brought his
Spanish-speaking church to the Los Angeles airport in the
middle of the night to meet the parents with hugs and ta-
males. In the morning, volunteers from a White Presbyte-
rian church brought the parents back to the airport to go
to places all over the country to meet their children. These
churches had experienced being part of a family of heroes,
united across their differences in a common love.

I hear people talk about healing the deep divides in our
society with words. I am amazed at the skill that must be
involved in making that possible. If that doesn't work in
your context, try our alternative – bringing people together
on common sacred ground to labor together in love for the
benefit of people in need. Of course, words are ultimately
required in our model as well – words that place experiences in the context of history and scripture, words that
enable people to see through each other's eyes. However,
we find that words in our case are seeds – seeds that grow
best when they fall into ground that has been watered by
the experience of right relationship.

Learn more about Matthew 25/Mateo 25: _matthew25socal.org_

Rev. Dr. Alexia Salvatierra is an author, professor, pastor, organizer, and activist. Her books include "Faith-Rooted Organizing: Mobilizing the Church in Service to the World." Learn more about Alexia: _www.fuller.edu/faculty/alexia-salvatierra/_

《9》

Healing Our Divides
From the Inside Out

Parker J. Palmer

For twenty-five years, the Center for Courage & Renewal (CCR) has helped people reclaim the wholeness that is everyone's birthright gift, so they can bring their identity and integrity more fully into their personal, vocational, and public lives. When people begin to "rejoin soul and role," they also begin to become agents of transformation in everyday life.

How is this kind of inner work related to healing our social and political divides? The answer comes clear when we understand how much of what's "out there" begins "in here." The pathologies of our social systems are, in part, projections of our personal pathologies, as when greed creates an economic system that allows the rich to get richer while the poor get poorer. The virtues of our social systems are partly projections of "the better angels of our nature," of our identity and integrity as members of the human race.

As Carl Jung taught us, when we fail to face what lurks in our own shadow—the *terra incognita* of every personality that terrifies us until we have the courage to enter into and learn from it—we project it onto others as a perceived moral deficiency (as when the rich justify their greed by accusing the poor of laziness).* That kind of projection, of course, is a major root of the "othering," scapegoating, and enemy-making that have undermined American democracy from the start of our quest for "a more perfect union."

So the quest for outer wholeness cannot be separated from a quest for inner wholeness. The retreats offered by the CCR support the former by facilitating the latter. Our "Circle of Trust" process creates a communal space where it's safe for people to listen to their own truth—including that which is hidden in the shadow—and draw more deeply on its guidance for their lives.

The "operating code" for those retreats is beyond the scope of this essay. Much of it can be found in my book, *A Hidden Wholeness*, and at the CCR's website. Here I want to offer an orientation to what happens in these retreats in the form of a four-stage model that traces how we lose touch with our wholeness, and what it looks like to reclaim it.

It's a model I've found helpful in diagnosing and treating the painful condition known as "the divided life." When we live and work in a way that's incongruent with our identity and integrity, something will suffer: our life and work, our integrity, or all of the above. When we project our dividedness on the world around us, the world suffers, too.

Stage 1: We are born as integral beings, with no wall of separation between what's going on inwardly and the way

---

*Jung defined the shadow as the unknown dark side of the personality. According to Jung, the shadow, being instinctive and irrational, is prone to psychological projection, in which a perceived personal inferiority is recognized as a perceived moral deficiency in someone else. https://en.wikipedia.org/wiki/Shadow_(psychology)

we present ourselves outwardly. Infants and young children are simply here as who they are, able in an instant to turn from rage to joy. They have no inner voice asking, "Is it OK for me to express this feeling to the world around me, or should I keep it tucked away in order to stay safe?" Kids are who they are, to either the delight or vexation of the adults around them!

Stage 2: Soon enough, children learn that it's not always safe to show up in the world as they are. Some, sadly, learn this at home. But almost everyone learns it at school, where it's usually unsafe to let yourself be known at depth. If you do, the punishments can range from loss of popularity, to being shunned, to being assaulted. A lot of LGBTQ+ folks have harrowing stories about this, but all have some experience of hiding out in a self-protective way.

Unfortunately, our educational system tends to make the wall behind which we hide grow higher, wider, and thicker. It's rare to find curricula that focus on the student's inner life, curricula rooted in Socrates' ancient maxim that "The unexamined life is not worth living." In the United States, education is about mastering knowledge generated by others, and developing the skill to use that knowledge to impact the external world. In most cases, the higher one goes in education, the farther away one drifts from self-knowledge.

Stage 3: Some people live a walled life until they die because it keeps them "safe," in the way an animal in captivity is "safe." But others reach a point where the divided life becomes so painful that something must change.

More than a few of us wake up in midlife with a sense

that we are living far from the wholeness with which we arrived in this world. So we seek to "center" our external lives, our words and actions, around the truths and values we hold most deeply within. Let this illustration—where a strip of paper has been formed into a circle by joining its ends—serve as a visual of what it means for our outward life to be "centered" around our inward life:

This stage of the journey toward an undivided life is an advance over to the earlier "walled" stage, where there is no effort to join or synchronize the inner and the outer. But as the visual makes clear, this circle is still a wall that looks like life in a "gated community." Too often, the message is, "You can join me inside this sacred space if you think and believe as I do. But if you don't, I'm going to keep you outside the wall." This prevents us from living our inner lives in a way that might impact the world, except as a silent statement of distrust.

Stage 4: The fourth stage of the journey toward an undivided life—a journey that never ends, but one we keep having to make as our conditions change—can be illustrated with the same circular strip of paper. Uncouple the ends, give one end a half twist, then rejoin the ends. You've just create a shape called a Möbius strip.

The Möbius strip has a fascinating property: it's a three-dimensional object that has only one side. Trace your finger around the surface, and *what appears to be* the outside of the strip segues seamlessly into *what appears to be* the inside of the strip, then back "out" again. You have to keep saying "what appears to be," because the Möbius strip has no "inner" and "outer." Its unbroken surface is con-

56

stantly co-created by the "inner" and "outer" as they segue into each other.

In a word, the Möbius strip is like life itself! Everything we put into the world from within ourselves helps co-create the outer world, for better or for worse. Everything the outer world puts into our inner lives helps co-create our inner worlds, for better or for worse.

The challenge for those of us who want to be agents of healing is clear. This co-creative process will be life-giving only if we are attentive and purposeful at every moment of inner-outer exchange. We must know what's inside us, shadow and all, and be thoughtful about what we put into the outer world. We must be aware and thoughtful about how we take in and process whatever the world sends back.

Living on the Möbius strip with full awareness is the adult equivalent of the wholeness of the child. Of course, wholeness is a lot more complicated for adults. This is not about "recovering the inner child"—it's about growing up. As adults, we travel the Möbius strip with our fears and tears, our gifts and our sense of responsibility. We can co-create heaven, or we can co-create hell. It's up to us, not just once but minute-by-minute, day-by-day.

I'll close with a brief story that illustrates the transformative power of the quest for an undivided life. I once facilitated a three-day retreat for twenty-five physicians, creating a safe space for tough and tender conversation. Among other things, we invited them to explore those painful moments when a patient dies while under their care. As we talked, one physician spoke up and said, "The rules of the hospital where I work have me on the edge of violating my

Hippocratic Oath several times a week."

There was a respectful period of silence, which allowed the speaker to feel the weight of what he had just said. Then he said, "You know, I've never said that to a group of fellow physicians." More silence, then he spoke again: "The truth is, that's the first time I've said it to myself."

Once your soul has spoken your own truth to you, it's very hard to live as if you didn't hear it. When this doc went back to work, he began speaking with colleagues, and learned how many of them were as troubled as he was. Together, they lobbied the administration for systemic reform.

Among other things, they created a penalty-free zone for the acknowledgment of honest medical errors. This will encourage the collection of information that can lead to systemic checks against hospital-induced injury and death, bringing the system into deeper alignment with the Hippocratic Oath to "do no harm."

If we want to repair broken institutions and broken relationships, we can't afford to ignore the inner work of overcoming the divided lives we so often lead. Imagine twenty years from now. The educational and religious institutions that help shape our lives have spent that time taking people on an inward journey toward the undivided life. What might our world look like then?

Parker J. Palmer is a world-renowned writer, speaker and activist who focuses on issues in education, community, leadership, spirituality and social change. He is Founder and Senior Partner Emeritus of the Center for Courage & Renewal. His many books include "A Hidden Wholeness: The Journey Toward an Undivided Life" and

WAYS YOU CAN GET INVOLVED

"Healing the Heart of Democracy: The Courage to Create a Politics Worthy of the Human Spirit." Learn more about Parker J. Palmer: <u>couragerenewal.org/parker/</u>

Learn more about The Center for Courage and Renewal: <u>howtohealourdivides.com/the-center-for-courage-and-renewal/</u>

«10»

ROOTS OF JUSTICE

Calenthia Dowdy

While glancing through articles at the digital magazine *TheGrio.com*, my eyes landed on an interview with The Lucas Brothers. They're twins who write, create, and perform standup comedy, and most recently wrote and produced the film *Judas and the Black Messiah* about the 1969 FBI murder of 21-year-old Black Panther Fred Hampton. The Lucas Brothers are young, Black visionaries with an incredible education, having attended the best universities and law schools. Both wanted to make a difference by bringing real justice to their communities as lawyers. Two weeks before graduation from a prestigious law school, both decided to drop out. They said law school was hell, and they weren't talking about academics or rigor. They were talking about substance: "...we already had a pretty antagonistic relationship to the law so once we got to law school it became even more apparent that this institution isn't built for African Americans, in fact it's built as a tool to oppress African Americans."* (The Lucas Brothers) The law was all about the systemic and structural continuation of

---

* *https://thegrio.com/2021/02/26/the-lucas-brothers-on-dropping-out-of-law-school-it-was-hell/*

white power and the ongoing oppression of African American people.

Well, I immediately thought, that sounds just like the church and American Christianity. In fact, the substantive issue with the majority of American institutions is that they were envisioned and created with white people, more specifically white men in mind. Moreover, the goal of these great institutions was/is the maintenance of white supremacy. It was one of the reasons Black people in the U.S. had to diligently work at starting their own institutions like schools, colleges, and churches. The other reason was that due to Jim Crow and other unjust laws, Black people were not permitted to attend white schools, colleges, and even churches.

After having taught at a white Christian college a number of years and feeling like a piece of left-over uneatable food ready for the garbage pail, I had to figure out what was happening with me. Why did working in white institutions, even the Christian ones, leave me feeling worthless, sad and horribly depressed? Eventually, I attended a Damascus Road anti-racism analysis training and that training became my sigh of relief, my aha, my liberation. Everything began to make sense as these incredible and insightful trainers gave language, explanation, validation, and affirmation to my experiences and feelings. I felt seen. I wasn't alone or insane. I felt compelled to join this team and become an anti-racism trainer too.

Roots of Justice, Inc. (ROJ) is an anti-racism analysis training program that was born within the church. ROJ was founded under the name Damascus Road in 1995 by Tobin

Miller Shearer and Regina Shands Stoltzfus, two Mennonite church leaders, a white man and an African American woman. Damascus Road referred to the biblical story of Paul, first known as Saul, who was on that road traveling to get official papers from official institutional leaders to capture and imprison any followers of that man called Jesus. Saul was on a mission to protect his religious and cultural institutions.

Meanwhile, Saul was still breathing out murderous threats against the Lord's disciples. He went to the high priest and asked him for letters to the synagogues in Damascus, so that if he found any there who belonged to the Way, whether men or women, he might take them as prisoners to Jerusalem.

As he neared Damascus on his journey, suddenly a light from heaven flashed around him. He fell to the ground and heard a voice say to him, "Saul, Saul, why do you persecute me?"

"Who are you, Lord?" Saul asked.

"I am Jesus, whom you are persecuting," he replied. "Now get up and go into the city, and you will be told what you must do." The men traveling with Saul stood there speechless; they heard the sound but did not see anyone. Saul got up from the ground, but when he opened his eyes he could see nothing. So they led him by the hand into Damascus. For three days he was blind, and did not eat or drink anything. (Acts 9:1-9, NIV)

Damascus Road was born from a core belief that for most of us, especially those who call ourselves Christian, it takes a blinding encounter with God for real transformation to happen within ourselves and within our institutions, especially for white Christians who unknowingly, and knowingly, support white supremacy. You cannot serve God and white supremacy.

Another core belief within Damascus Road is that in order to heal our divides we can't ignore institutions. White people focus on interpersonal relationships for the healing of racial divides, but Black, Indigenous, People of Color (BIPOC) know that much of the trauma and life altering harm comes through institutions. It is the policing institution that showed up at 2020 Black Lives Matter protests in riot gear with weapons drawn, but barely showed up and barely drew weapons at an actual riotous attack, January 6, 2021 on the nation's Capitol building. It is the housing and banking institutions that draw red lines around certain neighborhoods calling them high risk and loan adverse. It is the health care institution that has historically used Black bodies as test subjects without their knowledge or consent (for example, the Tuskegee syphilis experiments, the HeLa cells from Henrietta Lax, gynecological experiments, and so forth). Today, health system data reveals that white medical providers don't listen well to Black patients, underestimate Black pain, and give less than stellar care to their Black patients when compared to white patients. And then there is the Christian church that tried to convince Black believers that their lot in life was to be the perpetual servants of white people because God designed it that way (the so-called curse of Ham and other such offenses). Phrases heard in churches around the country, "natural order" and "God's ordained hierarchy" are triggers for me today.

Institutions can be dangerous.

In 2011 Damascus Road formally split from its church birthplace and went independent. A name change was needed, and Roots of Justice was born. ROJ continues to be committed to our core values but we don't only serve churches or religious organizations; we have broadened our reach to all people, institutions, and possibilities. Our emphasis is still on institutions and racism. Much of the healing involves acknowledging that institutions, not just people, are racist. The exhales in the room that we see from people of color are always so familiar. It's the same exhale that came from many of us trainers years earlier at the realization that you are not the misfit or the problem struggling to survive in white institutions or at the realization that the institution was not designed for you to thrive or survive. For BIPOC people in the training that is the beginning of healing.

For well-meaning white people in the training space, it can be jarring and a bit traumatizing. The knowledge that you and your BIPOC colleagues are not on the same journey and are not having the same or even similar experiences in the same institution can be bewildering. It's difficult to come to grips with the fact that perhaps you're doing so well because you're on a moving sidewalk and your BIPOC colleagues are on an unending jog up many flights of stairs. The institution works for you, and against others. However, once they get past the pain, denial, tears, and anger, the real work of transforming the institution can begin. Institutions have public legal policies and procedures, and also private or *ghost* policies and procedures. *Ghosts* refers to policies and procedures only revealed to a few in the organization, usually white people, to help them get ahead.

Structural and systemic transformation is a long and steady process. Transformation doesn't happen overnight.

WAYS YOU CAN GET INVOLVED

If current longstanding institutions can be transformed we are here to help transform them. However, I would be remiss if I did not mention many critics who say you can't change institutions that have been racist and oppressive since their inception. The famous Audre Lorde said, "The master's tools will never dismantle the master's house." We say that we are not using the master's tools. We're using freedom tools. And time will tell.

For Roots of Justice consultation and training, email us at roots@rootsofjusticetraining.org and check out our website: www.rootsofjusticetraining.org

And Facebook page where we livestream often: Facebook.com/RootofJusticeInc

Rev. Dr. Calenthia S. Dowdy is Director of Faith Initiatives at FIGHT and has held roles as a college professor and chaplain, a youth pastor, and facilitator for racial justice workshops. Learn more about Dr. Calenthia Dowdy: fight.org/fight-staff/calenthia-dowdy/

Learn more about Roots of Justice: howtohealourdivides.com/roots-of-justice/

Troubling the Waters

Two Approaches to Creating a More Beautiful World

Rev. Brandan Robertson

Binary thinking is usually a sign that we're not looking at something closely enough. In my experience, there is almost always a middle path or a third way in every disagreement or problem that we face that actually leads us more effectively towards the end that we desire. Yet in our era, binary thinking has become our standard mode of operation. You're either a Democrat or a Republican, and anything in between or outside of that is viewed with suspicion or disdain. You're a progressive Christian or you're a fundamentalist Christian. You're for us or you're against us. You vocally oppose them or you're in alignment with them. Sometimes, binaries do exist: there are some moral situations, for example, where there is a clear right and wrong. But more often than not, in most of the situations we find ourselves in, we'd be wise to heed the advice of the Sufi Mystic Rumi: "The middle path is the way to wisdom."

One of the areas that I have learned the importance of the middle path is in my own attempt to work for a more beautiful and whole world. I have spent almost a decade in the fight for LGBTQ+ inclusion and equity both within the Christian Church and within societies around the world, and in such spaces there is usually a bias towards one of two strategies for creating change: activism or advocacy.

Those who believe in the methodology of activism are usually convinced that the way to create change in any system is to use force – not necessarily violence, but the force of collective voices speaking up, shining a light on injustice, and not quieting down until something changes. The path of activism believes in confronting injustice head on, flipping tables and making a scene in order to expose evil wherever it may be hiding. The sacred path of the activist is often a costly one, because in speaking up and exposing systems of injustice, activists put themselves on the front lines and confront immoral power brokers face to face. Activists take pride in their fearlessness as they bravely and boldly do what needs to be done for change to happen swiftly.

Within almost every context where change is being sought, there are usually others who feel called to take a different approach – these are the advocates. Advocates are usually not interested in the confrontational posture that activists take. They believe, instead, that a more diplomatic approach is the most effective strategy to create change. Advocates are those who engage in "heart and mind change" work, through cultivating conversations behind the scenes with those who hold beliefs or support policies that they find to be immoral. Through conversation and the power of interpersonal relationships, advocates often help lead the power brokers on a path of subtle but substantial shifts in their posture, ultimately leading to systemic change that takes place over a longer period of time.

In every major social movement in modern history, both approaches have been crucial to creating social change. And in every modern social movement, these two approaches have usually opposed one another. Each respective "group," in the midst of a moment of conflict, believes the other is somehow impeding the effectiveness of the movement they are a part of. The activists see the advocates as sell-outs for engaging with the very people responsible for the injustice they're opposed to. And the advocates see the activists as hurting the cause by further entrenching the people they're trying to change in their harmful ideologies as they demonize the "radicals" who are opposing them. Instead of seeing each other as essential to a strategy for creating change, infighting between these factions usually slows down the potential for progress. But in the change that I have witnessed over the past decade, both are absolutely essential. The ancient words of Ecclesiastes 3 begin, "For everything there is a season, and a time for every purpose under heaven" (3:1 KJV). In every movement of justice, there is a time and place for the strategies of both the activist and the advocate in cultivating meaningful change.

Without the advocate's willingness to reach across the divides and engage even those who are perceived as their "enemy," it remains difficult to effect any true change of heart. Only when we're in proximity and relationship with those who are different from us can we gain the trust and empathy needed to begin reshaping their perspective. This work oftentimes puts the advocate in a vulnerable space – it's a fearful thing to sit across from an enemy. Yet only through this process of humanization can we move beyond mere ideological debates to a deep conversation about our different perspectives on the world.

In 2015, I had coffee with a prominent anti-LGBTQ+ evangelical denominational leader. This leader had just spoken at a conference the day before and declared that LGBTQ+ people were sinful and their attempts to be included in the church should be resisted – and here I was, an ex-evangelical openly gay pastor sitting with a man who didn't believe I could even be a Christian, let alone a pastor. During the course of our 45-minute meeting, I asked that we keep theology off the table. We weren't here to debate, but to get to know one another. I shared my experience of being bullied and threatened by religious leaders in his tradition, and my struggle simply to live into my calling as a minister of the gospel. He shared his own sense of fear about the perceived agenda people like me had to fundamentally change the church and force him to do things he didn't believe in.

By the time the conversation ended, this leader wasn't LGBTQ+ affirming and in fact, he still isn't to this day. But what had started was a real conversation between a LGBTQ+ Christian and an evangelical leader, and my sexuality moved from being a mere ideological debate to an incarnated reality for him. Since that first coffee, we've talked a few times and the fact is this leader has shifted his tone and approach to the topic of inclusion – I don't think our coffee is to credit for this slow shift, but I do believe it helped move him ever so slightly towards a less toxic and more affirming posture on the issue. That is real and substantive change.

Then there is the important role of the activist. Without their willingness to speak up against harmful ideologies and to shine a light on dangerous behaviors of leaders and organizations, injustice would surely flourish in the church and in society. Activists sometimes find themselves speaking against institutions and individuals that they used to identify with, and oftentimes this "burns bridges" as the activist seeks to hold them accountable. But to the activist, this cost pales in comparison to the harm that would be done if individuals and organizations are left unchecked.

Fast forward to 2017, and I found myself in the opposite position to where I was in my previous story. I was at the general conference of the same evangelical denomination of the leader I had coffee with, but this time as part of an effort to expose the increasingly abusive posture of this denomination towards LGBTQ+ people. I was with an organization who had purchased billboards and flew in dozens of us activists to help canvas the folks attending the conference with literature about how extreme the denomination's position on LGBTQ+ issues had become. I also found myself sitting in sessions and tweeting out the horrendous things being said from the stage, garnering significant media attention and putting pressure on the leaders of this conference. Eventually, because of the oppositional stance I was taking and the spotlight I was placing on the conference, I was escorted out by security and had my registration revoked.

Now, this level of activism was elementary compared

to what many activists are faced with. The consequences are often far higher than being removed from a conference. But the point is this: when the denomination continued to move in more extreme and harmful ways in their posture towards LGBTQ+ inclusion, I realized that advocacy wasn't enough. They needed to be called out and pressured to change. The precious lives of LGBTQ+ youth in their congregations were on the line, and those young people deserved more than a few coffee meetings. They deserved to have people standing up and defending them publicly.

There is a time and a season for both advocacy and activism. Most often, they should be occurring simultaneously. Sometimes, we may be called to be advocates to people and places where our experience gives us a unique ability to build relationships and shift perspectives. Sometimes, we may be called to be activists, making noise, burning bridges, and stopping injustice from occurring in real time. Both approaches are crucial to creating lasting change in our world and to following a radical rabbi who engaged in *both* activism and advocacy throughout his ministry. Christians should always be seeking to raise our voice and build relationships across divides – because this is how we will transform the world.

Rev. Brandan Robertson is a noted author, activist, and public theologian, working at the intersections of spirituality and social renewal. His many books include "True Inclusion: Creating Communities of Radical Embrace" and "Nomad: A Spirituality for Traveling Light." Learn more about Brandan: brandanrobertson.com/

«12»

IT BEGINS WITH HUMILITY

Shane Claiborne

I met a man in Texas once who came up after a speaking event. He confessed to me, "I am a redneck. A gun-toting, whiskey drinking, pick-up-truck-driving redneck." Then he continued, "But I've been reading your books, and they have messed me up. I wanted to ask you to pray for me. I'm a recovering redneck now." We hugged. And we prayed together.

Any attempt to heal the divides among us requires humility and grace... from all of us. I've always liked that Scripture that says we are "working out our salvation with fear and trembling" (Philippians 2:12). Spiritual conversion is not about a moment, but it is about a movement within us. A continual shaping that God is doing over time.

One of the things that can help us have a bit of grace with others is to think of the grace that has been extended to us. Few of us would agree with our own selves if we met up 10 years ago. I think of who I was 30 years ago, and sometimes wonder how much patience I would have if I met my old self and started having a substantial conversation about politics or justice. After all, I am a bit of a recovering redneck myself. That gives me a little patience with others who are also a work in progress.

One of my favorite quotations from Henri Nouwen is this one: "In the face of the oppressed I recognize my own face, and in the hands of the oppressor I recognize my own hands." He goes on to say when we see another person's ability to torture we know that we are capable of that same evil, and when we see someone's capacity to forgive and heal, we know we have that same capacity inside of us.

For this reason, we can celebrate the fact that God's love is big enough to set both the oppressed and the oppressors free. God is healing the victims and the victimizers.

I can remember an event overseas many years ago where I was, perhaps too pretentiously, winsomely joking about televangelists... only to find out that one of the women in the audience had a powerful conversion experience from watching a TV preacher. Experiences like that make you step back and think twice about limiting God or judging others. As I once heard a preacher say, referring to the biblical story of the donkey that speaks to Balaam: "God spoke to Balaam through his ass... and God's been speaking through asses ever since." So if God uses us, we shouldn't get too proud of ourselves. And if we meet someone we think God could never use, we better think twice.

Self-righteousness is toxic. And it takes on many different forms. There are self-righteous fundamentalists that pride themselves on their own piety. Growing up, I became very familiar with Christians who "don't smoke, drink or chew... or go out with girls that do." The purity culture frowned upon the secular world. But that is only one manifestation of it.

There is another version of self-righteousness I've become all too familiar with – in progressive circles. Many activist friends, and myself included, are prone to a self-righteousness that frowns upon people who drive SUVs or use Styrofoam cups or wear brand names from corporations that use sweatshop labor.

We must take our moral convictions seriously, but we also have to beware of the danger of building our righteousness in contrast to another person's wrongness.

Jesus did not just come to make "bad" people "good." Jesus came to bring dead people to life. Jesus didn't come to give us guilt but to give us life. And there are a lot of people who are moral, but mean. They may live responsibly but aren't much fun to be around.

I'd rather hang out with a humble conservative than a self-righteous liberal. And I'd rather hang out with a humble liberal than a self-righteous conservative. Humility is life-giving. And self-righteousness is always toxic.

It has become clear to me that we can build community, and movements, by isolating ourselves from those we disagree with. And we can also build movements that are open and inviting, seasoned with grace, even for those with whom we disagree.

It begins with humility. GK Chesterton was once asked what is the biggest problem in the world, the biggest obstacle to progress. And he answered with his characteristic wit, "I am."

The word humility shares the same root as human. They come from the word "humus" which means earth… which incidentally is where we also get hummus which some folks think tastes like dirt. It refers back to the fact that HUMans are made from the humus, the dirt... which God breathed life into. God makes beautiful things out of dirt. Always has.

That's the posture that invites others to the table.

Jesus tells a remarkable story about two folks praying. "Two men went up to the temple to pray, one a Pharisee and the other a tax collector. The Pharisee stood by himself and prayed, 'God, I thank you that I am not like other people—robbers, evildoers, adulterers—or even like this tax collector. I fast twice a week and give a tenth of all I get.' But the tax collector stood at a distance. He would not even look up to heaven, but beat his breast and said, 'God, have mercy on me, a sinner.' I tell you that this man, rather than the other, went home justified before God" (Luke 18:10-14 NIV).

The Pharisee, a member of one of the sects of Judaism that made up the religious elite in Rome's empire, boasts of his religious devotion and moral obedience, thanking God that he is not like the "evildoers." Then there is the tax collector who stands at a distance and dares not even look up to heaven. He just beats his chest and says, "God, have mercy on me, a sinner," and it's that tax collector, rather than the Pharisee, who goes home justified before God.

I'm convinced that the world is looking not for Christians who are perfect but for Christians who are honest. And the problem is that we haven't been honest, and we have pretended that we are perfect. The church should be a place where imperfect people can fall in love with a perfect God.

That stuff Jesus warned us to beware of, the yeast of the

Pharisees, is so infectious today in the camps of both liberals and conservatives.

Jesus consistently challenges the "chosen" and includes the excluded. His harshest words like "brood of vipers" were reserved, not for irreligious people on the margins, but for the self-righteous religious elite at the center of power, whose religion was toxic and oppressive.

Rather than separating ourselves from everyone we consider impure, maybe we are better off just beating our chests and praying that God would be merciful enough to save us from this present ugliness and to make our lives so beautiful that people cannot resist that mercy.

It all reminds me of this quotation from one of the leaders of the early church: "We who formerly hated and murdered one another now live together and share the same table. We pray for our enemies and try to win those who hate us." That was Justin (martyred in 165 AD). He went on to say, "We ourselves were well conversant with war, murder, and everything evil, but all of us throughout the whole wide earth have traded in our weapons of war. We have exchanged our swords for plowshares, our spears for farm tools... now we cultivate the fear of God, justice, kindness, faith, and the expectation of the future given us through the crucified one." Whoa.

This book is giving us glimpses of that humility, and showing us how we can heal divides and make room at the table for others.

Consider the circle of friends Jesus had. Think about his dinner table. He had a zealot and a tax collector (zealots killed tax collectors for fun on weekends). He had Pharisees and marginalized women eating together, which would never happen (at least in public). He will challenge the things that need to be challenged, both the sword of the zealots and the system of exploitation of the tax collector, and he will invite everyone to become a new creation. A new family.

There are a few magical times I have been able to experience this redemptive work of healing the divide. And there are a few special events I've even had the chance to craft, that bring people together to listen and learn from each other.

One of my early, poignant memories of redemptive, reconciling love in action was from Dr. John Perkins, one of my close friends and mentors over the past 30 years. John is the son of a sharecropper. His mother died at birth. He went to jail, was tortured and brutalized by police. His brother was killed in the struggle for racial justice, by police. And yet, at one point, John heard about a leader of the KKK who had a stunning conversion and change of heart. They became friends, and eventually wrote a book together (entitled *He is My Brother*).

Over and over I've encountered stories like that. I think of my friends in Iraq who started a movement called "Preemptive Love."*

Convinced that violence only adds fuel to the fires of hostility, their motto became: "Love now, and ask questions later." They began performing life-saving surgeries for Iraqi children, no matter who their parents were. At one

---

*Check them out here: *https://preemptivelove.org/*

point, there was a radicalized extremist, whose child was dying and they had the opportunity to save the kid's life. My friend Jeremy Courtney, founder of Preemptive Love, laughed as he told me, "We didn't have to pray long about that." They saved the kid's life, and they have story after story of how the walls come down when they extend that kind of preemptive love. On another occasion they had to fly a child to Israel for special treatment, and it was a Jewish doctor who saved the child's life. They got to tell his Muslim family about the Jewish family who saved their kid. That's the stuff that heals the world. The initial medical work of Preemptive Love eventually gave birth to a global community of peacemakers taking even greater bodily, spiritual, and psychological risks to preemptively love, serve, and learn from those on "the other side" all around the world. They are now on the front lines standing against escalating tensions and violence in Iraq, Syria, Lebanon, Mexico, Columbia, Venezuela, the US and beyond… getting in the way of violence and hatred in all its ugly manifestations.

It's these projects, like the ones in this book, that are healing the world. My own work as an activist has been shaped by stories like the ones in this book. Here are a few of the lessons I've learned.

We need to put names and faces on "issues." The way that we do that is by centering the voices of the people who have been impacted by injustice. Sometimes our biggest problem is not a compassion problem but a proximity problem. I don't know many people who have been argued into thinking differently on matters of justice… but I know many people who have been "storied" in. Not many people change their mind because they lost an argument. But many people's heads change because their hearts are changed or moved by another person's suffering.

So much of my work at Red Letter Christians has been shaped by this. We've hosted Faith Forums on different issues like abortion, gun violence, immigration, and the death penalty. At the heart of it all are real stories. Survivors of gun violence. Folks wrongfully convicted and sentenced to death. Immigrant families. People whose stories change hearts. Red Letter Christians gets our name from the Bibles that highlight the words of Jesus in red. We resonate with Gandhi when he was asked about Christianity and responded by saying that he loved Jesus, but just wished the Christians acted more like him. So at Red Letter Christians, we aspire to live as if Jesus meant the stuff he said. We want a church that acts more like Jesus. I hope you'll join us: _www.RedLetterChristians.org_.

And at the heart of my activism is a desire to move people's hearts, even through public marches, protests, and demonstrations. Dr. King used to say that we have to expose injustice and make it so uncomfortable that people can't help but respond.

Here are a few ways we've done that.

During the opioid crisis in Philadelphia, as our city was seeing over 1,000 lives lost to heroin, we had an idea. Moved by the kids in our neighborhood who had grown tired of seeing heroin needles everywhere, we launched a campaign we called "Need a Little Help" (pun intended). We put hundreds of heroin needles gathered from our streets into glass jars and delivered them to our city officials as a plea for help. Almost immediately, they began to respond. One city councilman said he put the jar on his shelf so he would not be able to forget how urgent this is. Before long, our Mayor declared a state of emergency with funding and a strategic plan to address it.

Around immigration reform, I joined hundreds of other activists around the country, including my close friends at the Christian Community Development Association, in holding a prayer vigil in the Capitol. To put a face on the issue, every speaker was accompanied by a DREAMer, a young immigrant activist who shared their story. We gathered over 3,000 dreams of immigrant families, written on little pieces of paper and we delivered them to the Capitol demanding immigration reform and a path to citizenship. We prayed aloud, and read the dreams until we were arrested. One of the officers arresting us mentioned quietly, "I'm with you. Thank you for what you are doing."

On the death penalty, we gathered at the Supreme Court with families of murder victims and with families of the executed to declare that violence is the problem, not the solution. We carried roses in two colors, insisting we want to remember the victims of violent crimes, and the victims of execution. We held 40 banners with the names of the more than 1,500 people who have been executed since 1976, when the Supreme Court allowed executions to continue. We were arrested for holding a banner that said "STOP EXECUTIONS" as Virginia carried out another execution. One of the things that made the event so powerful was having the victims of murder together with the victims of execution and to declare that killing is wrong, always wrong

Finally, one of the most powerful things I've been a part of lately is transforming guns into garden tools. We take donated guns to public demonstrations – turning them into shovels and plows. We are inspired, of course, by the biblical prophets Micah and Isaiah who cast a vision of "beating swords into plowshares and spears into pruning hooks." Together with my friend Mike Martin, founder of RAW Tools (and co-author with me of *Beating Guns*), we travelled all over the country, 40 cities, transforming guns into garden tools. But one of the things that made it so powerful was centering the voices of those who have been victims of gun violence. Folks who survived mass shootings. Police officers. Activists. Pastors. Gun-owners. Veterans. Mothers. Grandmothers. Children. All taking the hammer and beating on a gun to transform it. It was more than symbolic. It was sacramental. We had people share that they had actually killed someone. We had others share their trauma of surviving gun violence. It honored people's pain, and gave space for their grief. It was also hopeful. I remember watching with tears rolling down my face as Rev. Sharon Risher beat on the gun. Her mother was killed in Emanuel AME church in Charleston, SC, in the middle of worship. She named all nine of her loved ones as she beat on the gun. Afterwards, she tried to explain to me what it did for her, in her. She also smiled and said that everything she may have wanted to do to Dylann Roof (the shooter), she took out on that gun. It is the human stories that move us to action. We've even had people in the middle of a gun transformation ask if they can go home and bring back their guns to be decommissioned.

This is holy work we are doing. It begins with humility.

If you'd like to support more actions like the ones above join us at: _RedLetterChristians.org_, _CCDA.org_, _TheSimpleWay.org_, _DeathPenaltyAction.org_, and _RAWTools.org_.

Shane Claiborne is an author, and speaker, and activist. He leads Red Letter Christians, and is the author of several books including "Jesus for President: Politics for Ordinary Radicals " and "The Irresistible Revolution." Learn more about Shane: ShaneClaiborne.com

«13»

3 PRACTICES
FOR HEALING OUR DIVIDES

Jim Hancock and Jim Henderson

We've read about the *benefits* listening can bring to business and personal relationships. We've been *inspired* by civic leaders who model listening in their public lives. We've *praised* religious figures for seeking peace with their ideological opposites and we've said the world would be a better place if more people followed their examples.

But, of course, that's not enough, is it...

Being inspired by people who somehow manage to heal our divides — even *aspiring* to be the sort of people they are — comes nowhere close to *practicing* it ourselves.

Football, we've heard, is a game where 22,000 people who are desperately in need of exercise gather to observe the struggles of 22 people who are desperately in need of rest. And isn't that what we've done with listening?

On one hand, we pay attention as loudmouths and louts insult each other without regard for truth...because they reinforce our beliefs and values — or at least entertain us. On the other hand, we are deeply attached to celebrity empathizers who listen on our behalf. We pay them to model what listening looks like when it's well-produced and perfectly coiffed. We've come to think of listening as a rare gift granted to a special few instead of a gritty skill any of us can acquire with practice.

There's a big difference between *aspiring* to listen and *operationalizing* listening in ways that train us to become the sort of people who cross and heal relational divides repeatedly and on purpose.

Our first project together was a documentary film about a rabbi, an imam, and a born-again pastor in Peoria, Illinois who didn't walk into a bar but in fact did walk deeply into each other's lives. We took that story on because we were looking for a proof of concept.

Over many years, we had developed a hypothesis about how some people decide to cross the difference divide and how they actually do it, not just once, under special circumstances, but over and over again. Watching a hundred hours of interview footage for the movie, we were looking for evidence of a way of listening that doesn't turn into a shouting match and also doesn't require people to become experts in "the art of listening." We were looking for confirmation that there are best practices anyone can employ when listening to others who disagree.

As it happens, we ended up calling our movie *No Joke*. The first reason being that everyone we told about the project broke into a wide grin before we even finished describing the premise. They were way ahead of us.

The second reason we decided to call it *No Joke* was the seriousness of the three men in Peoria. They were unassuming, intelligent — funny as the day is long — and they were not kidding around.

The heroes of *No Joke* had counted the cost of their controversial friendship — each of them lost congregation members on account of their relationship — and, every time there was a conflict, they decided it was worth it to keep going, not because they agreed with each other about religion, or politics, or immigration, or even sports. They decided it was worth it because they came to respect, and then love each other.

To be clear, if we hadn't found the relational practices we expected to see in their friendship, we would've still had a good movie because their story is so good. But we did find the practices we expected. Talking in depth with the rabbi, the imam, and the pastor — and talking with their families and colleagues, mutual friends, city officials, and members of their congregations — confirmed our hypothesis.

After our three heroes watched the first cut of the *No Joke* movie, they gave us their blessing to structure the final half-hour around what we call The 3Practices. While they had never used that language before to describe their journey, they instantly recognized how the 3Practices were reflected in the weaving of their collective story on the screen.

They knew that, from the beginning, they had practiced *being unusually interested in each other*. That's Practice 01.

They recognized that, despite broad and deep disagreements on very important matters, each of them chose to *stay in the room with difference*. That's Practice 02.

Each of them — the Jew, the Muslim, and the Christian — knowing a great deal about the history of harmful encounters between some advocates of their respective religious traditions, nevertheless chose to *not compare their best with each other's worst.* That's Practice 03.

We'd seen these practices before — in relationships between opposing political figures, between leaders in labor and management, between people from antagonistic racial and ethnic groups, between women and men, between people who can't find agreement about much of anything, but still decide to respect each other as human beings.

What we hadn't seen anyone do yet was put the puzzle together to give us a clear picture of how these practices mesh to enable ideological opposites to 1) conclude that agreement is overrated and 2) experience in real life — a truth everyone recognizes once it's pointed out — that *when people like each other, the rules change.*

When we toured with the film and its three protagonists, we found that, as much as audiences loved the three men, what people really wanted to know more about was The 3Practices our clergy friends used to navigate their way across the difference divide to each other.

That's when we started experimenting with groups of invited guests in living rooms, restaurants, and houses of worship in one of America's most politically divided cities — Seattle, Washington. To be sure, the political divide is not equal: Seattle is overwhelmingly liberal. In practice, that means people who maintain their conservative views in Seattle don't do so by accident or because it's inherited from their parents.

So, when we got folks from the left and right together to talk about politics, morality, economics, immigration, racial equity, religious convictions, gender, law and law enforcement, culture wars and shooting wars, there was no shortage of strongly held, passionately stated opinions.

Before the two of us joined forces to start The 3Practices, we both spent decades studying how people form and communicate beliefs and opinions, handle conflict around deeply held values, and in some instances, change their minds.

Over the span of two years, we tested everything we knew on real-life ideological opposites in monthly gatherings in Seattle and in out-of-town 3Practice Events where audiences of just a few dozen or sometimes a few hundred people watched six or ten of their peers tackle tough questions in a public fishbowl setting.

We started with a three-minute clock for volunteers to give their opinion, followed by clarifying questions from others in the circle, but three minutes turned out to be too much time. Ironically when people weren't being interrupted, almost no one could fill three minutes. So we cut back to two minutes, finding it easy to give people another minute if they couldn't wrap it up before the alarm dinged.

We learned that anyone can listen for two minutes to someone they disagree with because they can see the clock – they know it won't go on for five or ten minutes – and they know they'll have a chance to ask questions soon.

We tested several approaches before settling on an insistence that each clarifying question begin with the phrase "I'd be curious to know." We re-tested nearly everything, and concluded, for example, that "I'd be curious to know" yielded better results than "I would be curious to know" or "I'm curious to know."

We started calling our gatherings *3Practice Circles* — because people look at each other across a circle and practice the practices with their allies and opponents.

We ruled out seeking agreement as the goal of 3Practice Circles. That almost never happens and when it does everyone is surprised, if not shocked.

The thing we found 3Practices Circles can reliably deliver is *clarity* – clarity and, maybe, understanding. And, it turns out, that's enough most of the time.

Another important adjustment was when we stopped calling ourselves facilitators and moderators and started referring to ourselves as *Referees* — because that's what we actually do in the Circle. We suspend our own preferences and behave as if we have no stake in the outcome of the game for the duration of the Circle. What we're concerned with is that the gameplay is fair and safe.

All this worked more or less from the beginning. We found that, if we created safe spaces to talk about unsafe things, people *wanted* to cross the difference divide, or at least watch someone else do it. And the Circles got better and better as we tested and refined the rules and roles that enable clarity between people with very good reasons to disagree with each other.

The rules are simple because the work is difficult.

A volunteer gets up to two minutes to address the Framing Question. Anyone may ask a Clarifying question that begins with "I'd be curious to know…" The volunteer gets up to one minute to respond to each Clarifying Question. The questioner may ask one followup if they want to know more.

The Roles are fairly straightforward. The Head Ref handles the clock, helps anyone struggling to find their Clarifying Questions, decides how close to call minor fouls, and works to ensure the safety of everyone in the Circle.

The Co-Ref is a spotter for people raising their hands to ask a Clarifying Question. Online, the Co-Ref keeps an eye out for what the Head Ref may be too busy to notice and interjects as necessary.

On occasion, the Head Ref asks the Co-Ref to trade jobs because the Head Ref is struggling or wants to take two minutes to address the Framing Question.

That's how the first 3 years of The 3Practice Circles played out and then came Covid!

When the Covid-19 pandemic shut down in-person Circles, we shifted to online Zoom Circles more smoothly than we thought possible, and overnight went from one or two Circles a month to two or three Circles a week. Also, our time zone reach expanded so dramatically that people from London, India, Spain, Australia, Qatar and Brazil began to drop in on our 3Practice Zoom Circles.

Now we train and certify other 3Practice Circle Leaders to do what we do in their networks, communities, organizations, and institutions. We're actively expanding 3Practice Circles so more people can experience seeking clarity with people who disagree with them. We're working to create a network of hundreds of 3Practice Circle Leaders, refereeing important issues in every time zone, so folks can always find an in-person or online Circle, like AA practitioners can always "find a meeting" and fitness devotees can find a place to work out regardless of where their travels take them.

It's not all rainbows and lollipops. There are times when the biggest takeaway from a 3Practice Circle isn't finding common ground but grasping the reality of our ideological opponents' intentions and, consequently, seeing how much more dedicated we need to be to make sure their plans don't go unchallenged in public.

Still, most of the time, we find what the rabbi, the imam, and the preacher discovered in Peoria. We find that we can choose to be unusually interested in each other, we can choose to stay in the room with difference, and we can choose to stop comparing our best with each other's worst – because when people like each other, the rules really do change.

There's a pithy book about how 3Practice Circles work on Amazon, called "3Practices for Crossing the Difference Divide."

Our website is 3PracticeCommons.com. There's lots more detail there, including upcoming 3Practice Circles and training, and some terrific videos of people practicing the Practices in 3Practice Circles.

Ask a question or leave a note at
www.3practicecommons.com/contact

Jim Hancock and Jim Henderson create spaces — and train others to create spaces — where people come to understand each other without being obliged to agree. Learn more about them here:
https://3practicecommons.com/our-story

«14»

CULTURE CARE

Mako Fujimura

Culture care is to provide care for our culture's "soul," to bring to our cultural home our bouquet of flowers so that reminders of beauty—both ephemeral and enduring—are present in even the harshest environments where survival is at stake. We may need to learn to cultivate these reminders of beauty in the same way flowers are cared for and raised. Culture care restores beauty as a seed of invigoration into the ecosystem of culture. Such care is generative: a well-nurtured culture becomes an environment in which people and creativity thrive.

At this point it will be helpful to gather the threads to find a working definition of my main terms. At the most basic level, we call something *generative* if it is fruitful, originating new life or producing offspring (as with plants and animals), or producing new parts (as with stem cells). When we are generative, we draw on creativity to bring into being something fresh and life giving.

We can also approach generativity by looking at its shadow, *degenerate*, the loss of good or desirable qualities (a term also frequently used of generations). What is generative is the opposite of degrading or limiting. It is constructive, expansive, affirming, growing beyond a mindset of scarcity.

One of Noam Chomsky's early definitions of "generative grammar" refers to the set of rules that can be used to create or generate all grammatical sentences in a language.* He was looking in human languages, as did my father in his work in acoustics, for a universal generative principle, an explanation of our ability to construct seemingly infinite phrases by switching out elements from a finite vocabulary and grammatical framework. Building on this, we might say that a generative approach will identify and model the "grammar" or conditions that best contribute to a good life and a thriving culture.

Discovering and naming this grammar, identifying and then living truly generative principles, is a process that depends deeply on generosity. This is because it requires us to open ourselves to deep questions (and to their answers), which is impossible when survival seems to depend on competing for scarce resources. But when we acknowledge the gratuitous nature of life—not least the world's inordinately diverse beauty—gratitude galvanizes us to ask and welcome questions that reach beyond our own context and experience. Artists at their best help us with such questions by presenting an expansive vision of life that reveals beauty in ever-wider zones.

Such a vision is by its nature a challenge to dictators and totalitarian regimes—a threat to those whose power depends on holding humanity at the level of survival or,

---

*See Noam Chomsky, *On Language* (New York: New Press, 2007).

worse, on eliminating diverse elements from societies. Artists and other generative people can sense dehumanizing trends quickly, and this is why they are often targeted by autocrats. But artists ultimately can reveal new facets of human flourishing even in the midst of tragedy or horror, pointing toward hope and meaning.

Another key generative principle emerges as we begin to escape the cramped thinking of a culture of scarcity: stewardship. Beyond mere survival, job function, bureaucratic specialization, or social roles is a wide scope of human concern and responsibility. We are all given gifts for which we all must care. Just as we are learning the importance of taking care of our environment to leave the earth healthy for future generations, so we must all care for culture so future generations can thrive.

Implied in this description is a measure by which to assess principles that claim to be generative: thinking and living that are truly generative make possible works and movements that make our culture more humane and welcoming and that inspire us to be more fully human. We can be comfortable, even confident, in affirming a cultural contribution as generative if, over time, it recognizes, produces, or catalyzes more beauty, goodness, and flourishing.

What emerges from generative moments is something new, transformed from its source, something that is both free and responsible to make its own ongoing creative contribution. I have on my farm a magnificent old pear tree. This tree has grown from a small seed. First, the seed died. It found welcoming soil and morphed into a tiny shoot. In time, with nurture, it came to full growth, a thing of beauty at many levels, all on a scale out of proportion to the original seed, and full of generative potential in its turn. The tree provides shade and shelter, flowers and fruit. It might provide wood for warmth or walls or works of art. It might contribute to a landscape or resist erosion. It might inspire poems or plays, paintings or photographs. It might spark a scientific discovery, host children at play, or lead a man or woman to reflect on the nature of life.

We can say that culture care is applied generative thinking. Culture care ultimately results in a generative cultural environment: open to questions of meaning, reaching beyond mere survival, inspiring people to meaningful action, and leading toward wholeness and harmony. It produces thriving crossgenerational community.

Working Assumptions

The framework of culture care rests on a number of foundational assumptions. Many resemble what one might expect when applying the principles of environmental stewardship (known in some circles as creation care) to cultural stewardship. I am assuming that efforts to restore the cultural environment are good and noble and that our efforts will benefit the next generation. I am assuming that an attempt to speak with people through conversations and questions that are outside the current cultural and ideological divide is healthy and will ultimately help culture thrive. In a polarized cultural reality that causes culture wars, even such assumptions may be challenged. The paralysis stemming from culture wars has decimated the fundamental trust in "the other," and we are unable to move beyond the conflict. A culture care stance brings in, despite this reality, a fresh new start, as culture care focuses on the promise of new creation, the potential of new types of communities.

As an artist and a Christian, I find the source and goal of beauty, of generative thinking, and of responsible action in the biblical understanding of what our lives are for. We find our creative identity in God. Genesis moments can be assumed simply because God is the great Artist, and we are God's artists, called to steward the creation entrusted to our care. The good news of the Bible is that in Christ we are journeying toward ultimate wholeness, integration, and well-being. We are becoming more fully what we were made to be, to the benefit of all creation.

But culture care and generative principles are not concepts only for Christian believers or churches or religious conversations. *Culture care is everyone's business.* Everyone can—and I gratefully acknowledge that many people from all sorts of backgrounds do— contribute to the common good. These conversations are open to all people of good will. To make culture inhabitable, to make it a place of nurture for creativity, we must all choose to give away beauty gratuitously.

Gratuitous can be a negative word, as in "gratuitous violence," but here I am using it to speak of intentionality, and even forcefulness, which, is necessary in our deeply fragmented culture. I will also be looking at how the reality of beauty can help integrate such fragmentation.

What if?

What if each of us endeavored to bring beauty into someone's life today in some small way?

What if we, by faith, saw each moment as a genesis moment, and even saw the current problems we are facing as genesis opportunities?

What if, instead of treating the independence and creativity of artists as problems to solve, we found in them opportunities for a new type of leadership in our current cultural flux?

What if artists became known for their generosity rather than only their self-expression?

What if art school became a place to train culture care agents rather than a filter that lets through only artists who can "make it"?

What if we considered our actions, decisions, and creative products in light of five hundred years and multiple generations?

What if we started to transgress boundaries by integrating our faith, art, and life—and speaking boldly about them?

What if we committed to speaking fresh creativity and vision into culture rather than denouncing and boycotting other cultural products?

What if we saw art as gift, not just as commodity?

What if we empower the border-stalkers in our communities, support them, and send them out?

What if we, like Mahalia Jackson, stood behind our preachers and leaders and exhorted them to "tell 'em about the dream"?

What if we created songs to draw people into movements for justice and flourishing?

What if we made things in secret, like Emily Dickinson, knowing that the world may not yet be ready for our thoughts?

What if we became custodians of culture, willing to be demoted for standing up for what is right but taking copious notes so we can challenge the status quo?

What if we assumed that relational and creative capital is infinite? What kind of effect would that have on our business practices?

What if we "gifted" photographs to share the light of the miraculous in people rather than "taking" photographs so that we can own and sell them?

Your "What Ifs"

Note down your own *what if* statements and share them with friends. Consider ways you can use these statements to help birth a plan for your community.

Makoto Fujimura is an author and a leading contemporary artist whose process driven, refractive "slow art" has been described by David Brooks of New York Times as "a small rebellion against the quickening of time." Learn more about Mako: makotofujimura.com/

«15»

A TALE OF TWO BUSES

A Vote Common Good Story

Vanessa Ryerse

I was at my 20th Bible college reunion the night the now infamous Access Hollywood story broke. It had been a long day and I was tired after making polite small talk with old Bible college acquaintances, reminiscing about the "old days" when we were not allowed to hold hands, or go to movies or to dance. Back then, both in Bible college and in the K-12 Christian school I attended for my entire childhood, I was used to lots of rules, especially rules for girls and how we must be modest and not "cause our brothers to stumble" by showing a glimpse of collar bones or anything above our kneecaps. I thought that night, as I drifted off to sleep, "Now this whole Trump nonsense will be over." I was certain that the people who had made all those rules for us through the years, the ones so concerned about our moral purity, would never give their vote to a confessed sexual predator.

Like so many others, I was horrified and disoriented the morning after the 2016 election to discover that 81% of Evangelicals, including many old friends and family members, did not find Trump's confession and behavior a deal breaker. That very day, my closest circle began plotting how they would oppose the Trump administration, but I was stymied, wondering if I could personally do anything about the national political disaster. I had grown up Republican and voted with "my team" for most of my life up until now, and I suddenly realized "my squad" had betrayed me and every other woman. I didn't know where I belonged and I certainly didn't know what I could do about it.

Many times during Trump's administration I would turn to my husband and ask, "Will there ever be a day again when our hearts aren't broken by this man?" As the saying goes, "Sometimes a breakdown is as good as a breakthrough." I was about to have mine.

August 3, 2019 all my kids were home: two college students, a high schooler and our youngest, a preschooler. We decided to go to Walmart for an annual back-to-school shopping day. I held up my phone to capture a selfie of all us together in my ugly mom minivan, and brought the phone down to see a "breaking news" headline on the screen. There had been another shooting.

This was El Paso. In a Walmart. Where families like ours were back-to-school shopping. And as the details of the violence came to light, my mind grew foggy with a grief that would not lift. First we heard that the shooter had laid out his guns in a literal homage to Trump, spelling out those five letters with his weapons. Then we learned from eyewitnesses that the shooter would save his ammunition, passing over white people, so he could use more bullets for brown bodies. That was what broke me.

Our third child is adopted. She is a beautiful Latina with

thick black hair and big brown eyes. She sings like an angel and her laughter is light. Among the little family alliances that inevitably form, Charleigh is everyone's person. She is a kind of salve when everyone is blistered with grouchiness. The horrific thought – if we had been in El Paso shopping at Walmart instead of Arkansas shopping at Walmart, that the shooter would pass over me and the other kids to take the life of our girl for no other reason than the color of her lovely skin – haunted me.

It haunted me to such an extent that I got on a plane and flew to El Paso to see the scene for myself. Vote Common Good had organized a Border Experience where we saw the ugly and invasive border wall, and we held a vigil at a makeshift memorial that spanned the length of a football field outside the Walmart store, closed off by crime scene tape. We stood outside the border detention facility where the ironically named "Homeland Security" was "protecting" us by separating little children from their mommies and daddies.

I went back to my room that night and wrestled with God. What could I, just a mom and a newly ordained pastor, possibly say to make a difference in the face of all this injustice?

"No one cares, God. Nobody is going to listen to me. I'm literally no one."

In that empty desert darkness, I heard simply and directly from God, "You haven't said anything yet."

So I began to talk. Because, like those little ones being detained, I know what it feels like to be a little kid in a dark place with grown-ups who are not safe. We casually called

Trump a monster, but he was not my first. That Christian school where I grew up had a monster under the stairs as well. His door was at the bottom of a hidden flight of stairs out of plain sight. Like Trump, he knew that he could grab and touch and move on the little girls who passed by his door. Like Trump, he did not see them as people... only as objects of his gratification. And when the men who ran that school found out – those good religious voters – they gave the man a cash "love offering" and quietly sent him on his way. I know this story is not unique, and I know there are many kinds of evil and injustice. But it is a special kind of evil to know something terrible is happening and choose to do nothing.

I joined the Vote Common Good bus tour, a self-described ragtag "band of merry-do gooders." Some of the people on the tour, like founder Doug Pagitt, had been on the bus since January; some, like me, hopped on and off the bus as life demanded. We traveled around the country in the weeks leading up to the 2020 election in outdoor, socially distanced events, to give religious voters the representation, sometimes permission, they needed to not vote reflexively Republican as they had been trained to do for so many years. Our events mixed music, poetry, storytelling, testimonies, stand-up, and sermons with the familiar feeling of a camp meeting. At these events, we saw conversions and re-commitments to voting for candidates that reflect Faith, Hope, and Love in their politics regardless of their party affiliation.

Night after night, I told my story. I told them how back then, when I was a girl in that school, we needed a pastor, a priest, some kind of protector. And how now, we need a president who can be a peacemaker to a divided country in the midst of a contentious pandemic. I implored them to please not give Trump the "love offering" of their votes. As a mother, I am motivated to help create a country that is safe for all my kids, all of OUR kids. And we cannot make it safer for children by making it more unsafe for women.

Our 2020 tour gave me the chance to get out from under the Access Hollywood bus and onto the Vote Common Good bus, helping to change minds and hearts of enough faith-motivated voters to elect Joe Biden instead of Donald Trump. As an organization Vote Common Good does many things. They provide training for candidates to be able to connect more authentically with faith voters about the things most of us hold in common. They are creating content via social media to deepen the public awareness of the dangers of Christian Nationalism and how to challenge baseless conspiracy theories. Vote Common Good supports Black Lives Matter, the LGBTQ+ community, gender equality, and justice for immigrants, and will continue to explore actions and events that foster the common good of all people who call the United States home.

But perhaps the most important thing Vote Common Good does to heal divides is to address the most deeply personal and internal angst within individuals, like me, who have been systematically trained for years to be good and quiet and obedient. We wonder,

"Am I the kind of person who participates in protests?

"Is THIS the time to speak up?

"Is this the way a Christian acts in the world?"

WAYS YOU CAN GET INVOLVED

Yes. The answer is yes. It's time to wake up, stand up, and speak up.

To heal those internal conflicts creates an un-self-conscious freedom to take action and lift all of our voices against injustice.

To vote for the common good is to step outside the limited boxes of political houses and into the shared green spaces we all want to see growing and thriving. At the crux, we ask how we can love our neighbors as ourselves, which is central to many faith systems, not just Evangelicalism.

You can get involved by following Vote Common Good on all social media platforms, supporting the organization financially, attending events that happen near you, listening to Vote Common Good podcasts and livestreams, and lifting up your voice with us as we craft new experiences together in the coming election seasons.

Vanessa Ryerse pastors Vintage Fellowship with her husband Robb. She is also a working artist, Etsy seller and avid gardener. You can find out more at vanessaryerse.com.

Learn more about Vote Common Good:
howtohealourdivides.com/vote-common-good/

«16»

AMERICA DOESN'T NEED FEWER ARGUMENTS

It Needs Less Stupid Ones

Seth Henderson and Erik Gross

The Better Arguments Project is based on the idea that the key to addressing division isn't for people to argue less, but to argue better. Too often, calls for unity or civility (while well-intentioned) can mean quelling disagreement or pushing issues under the rug. These approaches are mistaken because there are real, serious issues facing our nation that need to be debated. When we decline to share our true opinions or ignore our true differences for the sake of politeness, we are really doing two other things, perhaps unintentionally. The first is that we are failing to take accountability for shared problems. The second is that we are giving up our public discourse to the most polarized voices. These voices already have enough power and enough of a platform. To heal our democracy and our civic culture, we all must be productively engaging in the civic debates of the moment.

And besides, what's more American than arguing?

As Eric Liu, Executive Director of the Aspen Institute Citizenship & American Identity Program, wrote in The

Atlantic: "America doesn't just have arguments; America is an argument—between Federalist and Anti-Federalist world views, strong national government and local control, liberty and equality, individual rights and collective responsibility, color-blindness and color-consciousness, Pluribus and Unum."* Democracy itself is a perpetual argument. It brings new ideas to bear, allows policy proposals to be debated and examined, and gives every person a voice. But to make these arguments healthier and more productive, we need to change how we have arguments.

The Better Arguments Project began in 2017 as a partnership between the Aspen Institute Citizenship & American Identity Program, Facing History and Ourselves, and Allstate. Together, we set out to address the question: "What is a better argument?" In collaboration with advisors and communities across the country, we distilled our framework for having better arguments, which include the **Three Dimensions of Arguing Better** and the **Five Principles of a Better Argument**. While the Three Dimensions provide the background and context for every argument, the Five Principles highlight actions that we can all practice when engaging with those with whom we disagree.

The Three Dimensions of Arguing Better are **History**, **Emotion**, and **Power**. Today's civic arguments are rooted in all three, and these dimensions help shape all our views in one way or another. By understanding where each of us is coming from, we can begin to lay the groundwork for

---

* *https://www.theatlantic.com/politics/archive/2016/11/post-election-reconciliation/506027/*

empathetic and meaningful engagement across difference. So, we ask:

- History: What historical narratives inform our views?
- Emotion: What emotions do we feel when debating this topic?
- Power: How are power dynamics, implicit or explicit, shaping our argument?

There are some divides that may be too big or too difficult to cross, such as if someone's fundamental humanity is being denied or, as misinformation becomes increasingly relevant, there are divergent conceptions of reality. Each person should consider what is non-negotiable for them in an argument. If the difference of opinion is within an acceptable range, however, the Better Arguments framework can help improve that debate.

Once you've entered the better argument, there are Five Principles to practice in order to have a healthier debate:

- Take winning off the table
- Prioritize relationships and listen passionately
- Pay attention to context
- Embrace vulnerability
- Make room to transform

Take winning off the table can mean engaging with the person you're debating in order to learn, not to defeat them or convert them to your "side." This is arguably the most important step in a Better Argument, and for a lot of people, it might be the most difficult. But it is an important first step for creating a meaningful and intellectually honest conversation.

Next, it's important to **prioritize relationships and listen passionately** – try to think of your interlocutor in human terms, not just in terms of what their view is. An argument becomes "better" when we start the conversation with human connection and prepare to listen, not just advance our own points of view. Seek to learn more about a person beyond their opinion on the topic that you are arguing about and make a point to share more about yourself than just your own opinion. "You want to maintain that rapport, you want to maintain that relationship, even if you're going to have a pretty tough conversation," says Stacy Sharpe, Senior Vice President of Corporate Relations at Allstate.

When someone expresses a view you disagree with, it's important to **pay attention to context**. Instead of having a knee jerk reaction to what their view is – "How can you possibly think that?!" – try to pause and take a moment to ponder why they think that. Consider asking them about what influences have formed their opinions, whether it's news, popular narratives, or lived experiences, before moving forward. A person may not walk away from the argument agreeing with the other person, but hopefully each person will understand why and how the other person has reached their opinion on the argument topic and at least respect their right to hold to that position.

Embracing vulnerability is another difficult step for many people. Engaging in an argument is, by definition, difficult; it goes against many of our fundamental instincts. When debating someone, you might feel the need to pivot, change the topic, find commonality, or, worse, attack their personhood or character. But it's important to sit with the discomfort to make real progress. It can also be helpful to be open about your vulnerability, to admit your feelings of weakness or your own doubts in your argument. Embracing vulnerability should not solely be for the benefit of the person sitting across from you—it can help you get the most out of the experience as well. Consider if you would benefit from being honest about your own emotional vulnerability; you should not have to make yourself vulnerable simply to serve the needs of others.

Lastly, you must **make room to transform**. A Better Argument does not require parties to change their views or "meet in the middle." But to get the most out of the experience, it's important to at least be open to the possibility of change. That way you can gain a more nuanced understanding of the issue you're discussing as well as more respect and appreciation for the other person's point of view. If you're too unwilling to change, too unyielding in your argument, your debate will lack the potential to humanize and bring you closer to the person you are engaging with.

After developing our framework for constructive disagreement, the Better Arguments Project is setting out to change how we have arguments, one engagement at a time. We are working to educate the public on our approach and to facilitate conversations amongst people representing diverse viewpoints, as well as equipping them with skills to engage more productively across difference.

We are also working to embed our framework in the various sectors of civic life that make up our social fabric. We have resources for educators to bring Better Arguments to the classroom, workplace resources that can help managers and HR professionals create a culture of healthy dialogue, and resources to support communities building trust across divides.

There are several ways for the public to engage with the Better Arguments Project and help spread our work. First, you can attend one of our trainings, free and open to the public, which teach participants about our framework and ways to practice it in their daily lives. Second, you can use our free resources to help bring our framework to your own work, community, or context. Third, you can convene a Better Argument. We offer resources and support to help leaders and concerned citizens gather their community around an issue to debate. And lastly, you can practice these tenets and lead others in doing so. To heal our divides, we all need to be engaging empathetically and meaningfully with diverse views to contribute to our civic discourse.

Seth Henderson is a Program Manager at the Aspen Institute's Citizenship and American Identity Program. Learn more about Seth: betterarguments.org/about/

Erik N. Gross is a Program Coordinator at the Aspen Institute's Citizenship and American Identity Program. Learn more about Erik: betterarguments.org/about/

Learn more about The Better Arguments Project: betterarguments.org/our-approach/

«17»

Learning to be a Good Relative

Hearts and Hands

Shannon Crossbear

Greetings my relatives. "We are all related" is a phrase you hear frequently in tribal communities throughout the country. From an indigenous world view, we are all related. Learning to be a good relative requires one to spend time with one's relatives. One of my relatives said, "If you want to know about us, go to the library and read what is in the books; if you want to understand us, come and live with us."

Many years ago, one of the elders taught me that when you go to a new person, community, or land, go with a humble heart and a helping hand. Respond to what is asked, not what you think is needed. And always, always, offer something that will be helpful, be it food, water, or shelter. Offer a hand to work with or a hand to hold. It was solid advice then and is solid advice now.

There are many bricks in the wall that have divided us. As we dismantle the wall, we can use the material to build a bridge that finds shared spaces to do the work together. Bricks are made of concrete material; concrete actions can be taken to heal the divide. One can go beyond awareness of the inequities, acknowledgement of prior behavior, past the right and wrong of it, to actively participate in helpful and healing activities.

Healing activities. The word "healing" has differing cultural and contextual meanings. I have been taught that all healing takes place from the inside out, be it an injury, a wound, or an illness. As we think about healing, we might consider expanding our worldview to include the idea of approaching these deep divides as a wound. Healing must start from the inside and move out, first with the individual then, expanding out to families, communities, and nations.. Some injuries are more severe than others and may need more than one strategy just as wounds and illnesses have differing treatments.

Within an indigenous perspective, healing the divide or, as indigenous thought would say, healing the sacred hoop of humanity, requires all aspects of our human nature be attended to; *physical, mental, emotional,* and *spiritual.* I will be highlighting four Native American organizations that have created spaces for the shared concrete work to be done within these aspects. These organizations operate out of an indigenous world relational view, a view that embraces the idea that all things are connected. For example, one cannot think of the issue of murder and missing indigenous women without connecting it to the environment and climate conflict. One cannot think of economic development without thinking about youth suicide. The connections and inter-relational lines are part of the thought pattern that comes with a world relational view. A friend once explained it like this: from a eurocentric vantage point we live in a great house and that house has many separate rooms. From an indigenous viewpoint there is one house with only one large circular room. You will see this worldview reflected when you look at how, for example, the issues of clean water intersect with the concerns over child safety. The work each of these organizations does contributes to the overall healing.

Let us start with some of the *physical* aspects of healing. I chose to highlight **Honor the Earth** because they directly address issues around clean water and nutritious food. These are some of the most basic needs in Indian Country. The lack of access to potable water on tribal lands is a critical contributor to poor health outcomes. Recently, during the Covid pandemic many tribal people suffered as a result of lack of clean water. Climate justice, including food sovereignty and sustainable harvesting practices for food is a place where helping hands are needed. Honor the Earth expresses their mission as to create awareness and support for Native environmental issues and to develop needed financial and political resources for the survival of sustainable Native communities. Honor the Earth develops these resources by using music, the arts, the media, and Indigenous wisdom to ask people to recognize our joint dependency on the Earth and be a voice for those not heard. As a unique national Native initiative, Honor the Earth works to raise public awareness and raise and direct funds to grassroots Native environmental groups. They are the only Native-run organization that provides both financial support and organizing support to Native environmental initiatives. They have an active place for allies to contribute to the efforts in a variety of ways including, but not limited to, taking direct action, legal assistance, community organizing, resources development and education. They have partnered nationally and locally and are open to finding ways to ensure a collective future.˙(honorearth.org)

Moving into the *mental* aspects of our healing led me to look at how we define being of good mind. We have learned that cultural connections can aid us and encourage resiliency when we experience loss or trauma. Many arrows of risk are present in our tribal communities. It is important to build a strong shield of protection. **White Bison** provides some of the materials that can help. I became acquainted with White Bison shortly after the founder, Don Coyhis, began the organization. I was looking for resources. I was called to do some work in an adolescent juvenile detention setting. These young girls had found themselves confined to long-term detention, and I was called upon to provide some group activities around health and wellness. White Bison was piloting a curriculum called Daughters of Tradition. The curriculum was built upon teachings rooted in the values that were culturally congruent with tribal relational worldview. When I saw how the young girls responded and started to make different choices for themselves, I knew good work was being done.

Through White Bison, the Founder and President Don Coyhis, Mohican Nation, has offered healing resources to Native America since 1988. White Bison offers sobriety,

---

*Honor the Earth: *honorearth.org*

recovery, addictions prevention, and wellness/Wellbriety learning resources to the Native American/Alaska Native community nationwide. The term Wellbriety coined by White Bison describes overall wellbeing. It does not indicate merely the absence of drugs or alcohol, rather a further step in being on the path of wellness. White Bison has taken on the difficult discussions around healing intergenerational, co-occurring mental health and substance use, family disruption, and other issues that contribute to being unwell. Many non-Native people also use White Bison's healing resource products, attend its learning circles, and volunteer their services. If you find yourself drawn to servant leadership and the Wellbriety Movement, then please check out White Bison.*

When I think of *emotions*, I think of the heart. I think of the women as the caretakers of the heart. It is said that our human journey is over when women's hearts are on the ground. As I think about who is doing the most phenomenal work with wellness across "Indian Country" I immediately think of the **Native Wellness Institute** (NWI).

On the landing page under the heading of history it talks about having been founded in 2000. That is just the legal founding of the organization. The beginnings of this movement have been generations in the making. The Native Wellness Institute exists to promote the well-being of Native people through programs and trainings that embrace the teachings and traditions of the ancestors. The knowledgeable and dedicated leaders are women I have

---

*White Bison: *whitebison.org*

had the honor of meeting along my own journey. They have always been committed to making a positive difference for all indigenous peoples. Though they started in the United States, the reach of the Native Wellness Institute is worldwide. Community by community, relationship by relationship, they have built a movement that embraces cultural teaching as a pathway to wellness.

NWI is a leading provider of Native-specific and wellness-related training and technical assistance to Native people, communities, tribes, and organizations throughout North America. They bring together the most highly skilled Native trainers and consultants to share their knowledge and wisdom at large national conferences. They also offer smaller regional workshops in Native communities that improve physical, spiritual, emotional, and mental well-being. NWI is bringing about positive changes like no other organization of its kind in Indian Country. During the pandemic they offered daily power hours that allowed people from all over to participate and learn everything from the use of medicinal plants to healthy grieving. Witnessing lives transformed is certainly emotional work and cements the power of connection. Hands and hearts are important, and knowing that there are many non-Natives who work in a variety of capacities in agencies that serve or collaborate with Native American/ Alaskan Native Peoples, NWI provides specific training around being an ally in Indian Country.*

In most of our indigenous language, when we speak of

---

*Native Wellness Institute: *nativewellness.com*

children, we speak of the sacred ones. We are told to look upon our actions with the thought of how it will support the future generations. Every decision should be made with the next seven generations in mind. When we think about the *spiritual* aspect, we turn to the youth. Being youth-guided gives this next organization a level of credibility with those it seeks to serve. I have thirteen grandchildren and over half of them fall into the age range that The Center for Native American Youth is working with. I have seen firsthand some of the results of the work done around leadership, language reclamation, media presence, and increased visibility.

The **Center for Native American Youth** (CNAY) at the Aspen Institute is a national education and advocacy organization that works alongside Native youth—ages 24 and under—on reservations, in rural villages, and in urban spaces across the country to improve their health, safety, and overall wellbeing. All Native youth deserve to lead full and healthy lives, have equal access to opportunity, draw strength from Native culture, and inspire one another. Giving youth and young adults a pathway to express their leadership and support policies that ensure inclusion and voice in decisions that will impact their future are foundational in mending the divides. CNAY achieves this through empowerment and opportunities that include leadership, youth-led policy agenda, and youth-led narratives. Native youth are taking on everything from land stewardship to addressing the issue of the murdered and missing indigenous women.

CNAY has several ways you can engage and take actions

on issues that matter to you. IllumiNative, and the Native Organizers Alliance are two of the organizations that the center partners with, and they both also offer opportunities for allies. Consider where your efforts might be needed or your skills aid in the support of these young emerging leaders.*

When my siblings and I would fight, my parents would most times not intervene. They sent us off to "work it out." If we were not able to do so, then they would intervene. This was usually incentive enough because we had learned that the cost of not doing so was high. Usually, my father would come up with a difficult task we had to do alone. We could get no aid from the one we were quarreling with until we were done quarreling. Healing the divide is a difficult task. It is time to be done quarreling so we can get on with the task.

These four organizations are a start. They will lead to others, and the relationships will expand. Whether you are passionate about frogs or freedom, hydration or healing, entertainment or the earth, there is a place for your hands to work. Here in the middle of the divide, at the center of the wound, healing from the inside out.

Shannon CrossBear is an Ojibwe/Irish mother and grandmother, storyteller, and leader in traditional healing methodologies. She is an enrolled member of Fort William First Nation of the Lake Superior Ojibwe, which is located in Ontario, Canada. Learn more about Shannon: linkedin.com/in/shannon-crossbear-329ab712/

---

*Center for Native American Youth: cnay.org

«18»

BUILDING RECONCILING COMMUNITIES WITH ARRABON

David M. Bailey and Tiffanie S. Chan

There seems to be no end to the things that divide us. As Americans, our divides are significant, pervasive, and historical, and the global pandemic and racial reckoning of 2020 have served to turn the fault lines of divides into the deepest fissures we've seen in generations.

As a Black man born and raised in Richmond, Virginia, the former capital of the Confederacy, and as one who has been called to be a minister of reconciliation, I see two key causes for our deep, seemingly irreconcilable, divides. First, American Christianity has long neglected the peculiar and critical foundation for peace-making and reconciliation that the first century church practiced for 300 years after Jesus' death and resurrection. This is not an optional area for us as believers; rather, it is core to our calling as salt and light in the world. We are to be peace-makers, but we are desperately lacking in our prioritization of spiritual formation and discipleship in this area.

This leaves us ill-equipped to grapple with the second major piece that contributes to our current divisions — America's historical and pervasive racial caste system. Going back to the beginnings of chattel slavery and the violent colonization of native lands in the 1600s, our society has operated on a racial hierarchy that places white people superior to those of all other races, especially the black race. It is a spiritual principality that has been manifested economically, legislated politically, and affects us all relationally.

Because we have not done the foundational work of discipleship in peace-making and reconciliation, we have not developed the cognitive or emotional bandwidth to grapple with the complex and uncomfortable consequences of our national history. And so as each year ticks by, our divisions deepen and widen, and it becomes harder and harder to see our brothers and sisters on the other side.

Building Reconciling Communities

Such deep and entrenched divisions cannot be solved by a one-size-fits-all approach. People form institutions, and institutions form people, so we cannot focus only on individual transformation or rely solely on institutions to bring about change in our communities. We need the collective transformation of individuals, institutions, and communities in order to bring healing and deliverance to the world.

At Arrabon, we work to bridge these deep divides by equipping people and institutions to build reconciling communities. These existing communities, whether they are churches, universities, foundations, non-profit service organizations, parachurch ministries, or private K-12 schools, often feel the pain point of conflict and struggle that come with growing in diversity and awareness. The community leaders might have a strong desire for their community to better reflect the kingdom of God, but don't have a clear plan for how to get there. The people that the organization wants to serve may be feeling more hurt than helped.

Arrabon walks alongside these communities as a trusted friend who has walked this path before. We bring training, tools, and resources for the journey towards becoming a reconciling community. We work towards moving people and organizations along the transformative path from becoming aware of and acknowledging the depth of brokenness in our world, to actively participating in God's invitation to bring healing to the brokenness.

Five Pillars of a Reconciling Community

In our teaching and training, we use the Five Pillars of a Reconciling Community as both inspiration and benchmarks for holistic growth as a community.

1. Reconciliation as Spiritual Formation. While it may be difficult to recognize in ourselves, it's a sad truth that most Christians are more concerned with being right than with being righteous. But God is much more invested in our righteousness, as evidenced by the original transformative work of reconciliation — Christ's incarnation and sacrifice for us. So as we seek to heal the brokenness and conflict in our world, we must focus less on assigning right and wrong, and instead engage in self-reflection as we ask ourselves how we are in need of transformation. The practice of reconciliation is, first of all, internal work of spiritual formation that will then bear outer fruit.

2. Increase Your Community's Cultural Intelligence. It is not enough to simply learn about other cultures. In order to develop the skills for meaningful relationships across cultures and your ability to adapt to diverse spaces, you need to build curiosity, awareness, and knowledge about how values, thoughts, actions, and beliefs vary across cultures. Understanding your own community's culture, and the similarities and differences between cultures, builds the foundation for creating authentic spaces of hospitality where cultural wisdom and experience can lead your community to innovative solutions to struggles and conflicts.

3. *Learn Your Community's Diverse Shared Narrative.* When we hear the experience of another person within our community that differs significantly from our own experience, we are often tempted to dismiss or even doubt that person. However, the work of leaning in to the differences and listening to the "why" and "what" has shaped their experience and can help uncover wisdom and understanding.

4. *Participate in Cross-Cultural Collaboration.* This pillar moves us from theory to practice and allows us to experience the richness that comes from bringing different perspectives together to create something new. We will experience conflict and misunderstanding as we reach across cultures, but by digging into the principles we've learned earlier, we can also experience innovation and insight that we would have otherwise missed.

5. *Engage in Reconciling Culture-Making.* We are where we are today because of what happened yesterday. If we want to see a different tomorrow, we have to create new culture today. This final pillar is tied tightly to cross-cultural collaboration to create opportunities for innovation that make significant changes in your community.

In order to be transformative, all five pillars must be part of the foundation for a reconciling community. Transformative reconciliation requires the internal work of spiritual formation and discipleship, the interpersonal work of developing skills for conflict resolution and cross-cultural engagement, as well as the strategic work of creating intentional and lasting practices for communities pursuing reconciliation together.

Start Local and Build Outward

We believe that if you want to change the world, you have to start within your community. In Scripture, we see how Jesus had his inner circle of Peter, James, and John, who were 3 of his 12 disciples, who walked closely with him throughout his earthly ministry. In Luke 10, we see Jesus send out the 72 to proclaim the Kingdom. And throughout the Gospels we read of Jesus teaching and ministering to crowds of thousands.

By the same principle, we structure our organizational work around ministering to the needs of an institution's directional leaders (the 3), their staff (the 12), their key volunteers or next tier of people with institutional buy-in (the 72), and the community they serve (the crowd). At each level, we shepherd these groups to develop a clear vision of what it looks like for them to be a reconciling community in their context, as well as develop strategy for how to leverage their position to influence growth and progress for their community's journey towards reconciliation.

Join in the Journey

In 2020, in the midst of a global pandemic and racial uprisings across the United States, demand for our ministry grew more than 250%. As our team has worked to scale our ministry outreach to meet demand, we are intentional about creating entry points for people to join with us at whatever point they may be along their journey to reconciliation.

Many folks get introduced to what we're doing through friends, podcasts, or our study series, or they find us through the songs, albums, and worship resources created by the Urban Doxology Project. Our first invitation is to sign up to receive our newsletter for timely insights from me and our team.

If you'd like to be a part of the movement to build reconciling communities, we invite you to experience our trainings and resources for yourself and with your community. Whether it's a small group Bible study, or signing your team up for our Reconciling Community Transformational Journey program for organizations, our team and resources are ready to walk with you on this journey to healing and reconciliation.

Go Deeper in Partnership

As part of our own community-building, we encourage those in our crowd to dig deeper into partnership with us by Learning, Sharing, Hosting, and Giving. Many who join with us are already on the path of learning and awareness. But taking that next step to share with folks in their circle, even just one-on-one with a friend, not only serves to increase awareness and conversation about Arrabon and our offerings, but deepens the learning of the person who does the sharing. (Teachers know this! As students explain a concept to a peer, their own understanding is deepened and solidified.)

When a partner chooses to host, whether it's a Bible study, workshop, event, or documentary screening, they are doing more than simply sharing Arrabon materials with folks in their community. They are opening up the power of their personal networks to us, which creates the potential for powerful new relationships and impact.

Finally, we encourage partners to Give. While certainly our ministry has financial needs that need to be met, those needs are not the sole, or even primary, reason for this step. Giving of the wealth and resources we have been given, no matter how small, is a matter of spiritual formation. Jesus teaches us in Matthew 6:21, that wherever our treasure or wealth is, our hearts will be there too. While your money may be the tangible piece that you invest, your compassion and care and involvement in the things that stir the heart of God is what's truly important and desired.

A second reality about giving, in regards to race in particular, is that the economic manifestations of the American racial hierarchy are deep and wide. We encourage partners to give to local organizations that are doing the work of bridging racial divides in your area — consider organizations that invest in equitable housing and education, or create opportunities in art or athletics, or address food security through community gardens or accessible grocery stores. In what areas do you and your family have particular interest? Learn and invest in those who are doing the work to make those activities you love equitable and enriching for the people in your community that continue to suffer from the economic impacts of centuries of racism.

We did not simply wake up one day to a suffering world. These deep divides and painful wounds at the hand of our racial hierarchy have been centuries in the making. The choices that we make, whether it's to prioritize peacemaking in our spiritual formation or supporting Black-owned business and organizations, both form us inwardly and impact our community outwardly.

Partnering with Arrabon is a peace-making endeavor, and we urge you to explore ways that our work can speak into your own life and the life of your community to bring about the peace of the kingdom of God, on earth as it is in heaven.

David M. Bailey (Founder & CEO) & Tiffanie S. Chan (Director of Communications) are collaborators at Arrabon, a ministry that tends to the soul of leaders and communities to build reconciling communities for a broken and divided world. Access Arrabon's comprehensive training program for leadership teams, biblically-based study series for small groups, and cross-cultural worship resources to cultivate an organizational culture of reconciliation at arrabon.com.

Learn more about Arrabon at howtohealourdivides.com/arrabon/

«19»

THE JULIAN WAY

Discovering the Gifts
of Diverse Embodiments
Within All of God's People

Justin Hancock

The core value that lies at the heart of everything The Julian Way does comes from the 14th century English mystic, Julian of Norwich. In her revolutionary work, *Revelations of Divine Love*, Julian states, "All of God's creation is God's good creation." We at The Julian Way are an organization dedicated to education and empowerment with, for, and by persons with disabilities, or as we like to say, diverse embodiments.

The journey of The Julian Way began in 2013 as my wife Lisa and I were reflecting on an experience of trying to navigate a new Medicaid office right after moving to Dallas, Texas. We had been paying particular attention to the isolation and dehumanization that persons with disabilities often feel when trying to navigate state-based health systems. One day over bagels we began to dream about how the principles of intentional Christian community could impact the loneliness and isolation that so often predominates within the disabled community.

After several weeks of prayer and reflection, my wife and I took this concept to the leadership team of The Missional Wisdom Foundation where I was working at the time, living out my calling as a United Methodist Pastor. After we laid out our vision of a community where the disabled and able bodied come together and experience life with love for one another, The Julian Way was officially born.

Although The Julian Way took shape and was founded in 2013, it was a situation in the summer of 2014 that Lisa and I point to as our inciting incident for the force for social change that The Julian Way would eventually become. I was attending the 2014 conference of what was then known as The Summer Institute for Theology and Disability, now just The Institute for Theology and Disability. On the last day of the conference, to an audience packed full of persons with numerous disabled embodiments, a prominent theologian told the room that it's the church's job to speak for those with disabilities because they cannot speak for themselves. At that point at least nine of us with disabilities rolled, walked, or otherwise made our way out of the room. God began to say to me, "This is your moment. This is why The Julian Way is needed. We need disabled leadership in the church. If you don't do this I will find someone who will but nobody will do it like you will."

(The Institute is an organization I'm still proud to associate with to this day. Since this incident took place in 2014, they have made tremendous progress by addressing their shortcomings and actually including those with visible and invisible disabilities as presenters at their conference and in their overall executive structure.)

Building off of the momentum from that 2014 inciting incident, Lisa and I began to gather around us like-minded young adults with disabilities and allies for a series of community dinners at our home in Dallas. These community dinners were the beating heart of the early life of The Julian Way. Gathering folks of diverse embodiments around one table for good food and good stories allowed us to discover common purpose, the joy of friendship, and the common language of self advocacy that we still use to this day.

I remember one story from these dinners that will stay with me forever. Sally, a young woman dealing with Cerebral Palsy found her way to The Julian Way through a mutual physical therapist friend. Sally is a woman with a huge heart and much love to give the world. For a variety of reasons I won't go into here, she deals with depression and anxiety. Nicole is a woman that deals with a variety of sighted issues and has incorporated the sometimes joyous and sometimes difficult journey of her adoption into her story. Watching these two individuals connect and form relationships throughout the time of these initial dinners gave me such hope and optimism around the core message of empowerment that The Julian Way was trying to develop. Sometimes stories of empowerment begin simply when two people who would have otherwise not connected are given the opportunity to form a relationship and impact one another's lives.

We held The Julian Way dinners from early 2015 through the end of 2018. Lisa and I took a break when we were expecting our first child. Although we have not resumed this style of in-person dinner, I can still feel the soul of these early dinners in the way we try to journey with folks as we learn about and empower the telling of these individual stories and the discovery of the unique gifts that the persons we interact with have to offer God's larger world.

In conjunction with our early community development around a dinner table, I also was writing *The Julian Way – A Theology of Fullness for All of God's People*. This book takes people through a process of discovering how we talk about disability in the western world, an exploration of the early disability civil rights movement and the Americans with Disabilities Act (ADA), and discusses the way that the Christian Church has and continues to frame the reality of disability in sometimes positive but very often detrimental ways.

The book ends by using narrative theology to envision The Julian Way as a universally designed community where the able-bodied and disabled live together to effect change in their community and bring about a vision of the Kindom of God on Earth.

In 2018, as the book was being published, I was invited to give the opening sermon at the Eastern Pennsylvania Annual Conference of the United Methodist Church. The theme of the annual conference that year was built around empowering people with special needs. It was a huge honor for The Julian Way and our mission of advocacy and empowerment for those with disabilities to be highlighted in such an important space.

The future of The Julian Way is in many ways the future of people of faith and hopefully culture at large around the globe. Whether it is helping a student with special needs

obtain funding for graduate school, speaking at conferences and conventions around disability theology and civil
rights, or journeying with people through the individual
victories and struggles of daily life, the core mission of The
Julian Way has been and will remain that persons with disabilities do not just deserve to be a part of communities
of faith and our culture at large; rather, that if these voices
are not given a prominent place in our civic and religious
conversation then something deeply important and fundamental is missing from the human experience.

In July of 2020, The Julian Way had an opportunity to
begin developing more educational resources for both civic
and religious spaces, and increase its scope and vision for
disability empowerment. With the blessing of the Missional Wisdom Foundation, we took the opportunity to form
a new partnership with The Neighboring Movement out
of Wichita, Kansas. The background of The Neighboring
movement in asset-based community development, or
ABCD, fits hand-in-hand with the mission of The Julian
Way in helping persons with diverse embodiments discover their own gifts and graces.

Although it was challenging to leave The Missional Wisdom Foundation, the organization that gave us our start,
we could not be happier with where God has brought us
to. We are already developing three trainings that will help
both religious and civic organizations not just adapt to persons with diverse embodiments but rather learn to expect
people of various embodiments to be there in the first place.

In addition, we do a weekly blog focused on a disabili-
ty-related issue or theme, and we recently unveiled a disabil-

ity community and comedy podcast, "Palsys with Palsies," which looks at the world around us through a sometimes humorous, sometimes serious, but always socially-minded disability lens. We are a proudly self-funded organization with dreams and power to change the world. If you want to experience our work and engage with all we are doing, please visit us at *thejulianway.org* or follow us on Facebook *@thejulianway*, as well as, *@thejulway* on Twitter. We at the Julian Way are convinced that God is doing something, a paradigm is shifting, through the diverse people of the disabled community. We invite you to come join us and help create a world of fullness for all of God's people.

Rev. Justin Hancock is co-founder, with his wife Lisa, of the Julian Way, a ministry of community, advocacy, and empowerment for those with disabilities. He holds a MA in Christian Ministry from Perkins School of Theology, Southern Methodist University. Learn more about Justin: neighboringmovement.org/the-julian-way

«20»

THE COLOSSIAN FORUM

If the Holy Spirit Doesn't Show Up, We're Screwed

Michael Gulker

A decade ago, I was invited to lead a fledgling nonprofit that wanted to do something positive about the deep divisions within the Christian church. The Colossian Forum was created out of a recognition that the church was being forced to deal with controversial issues but was responding in ways that are less than Christlike. We're not talking about the quibbling over hymns vs. praise choruses or the color of the new carpet in the sanctuary. Instead, churches were faced with challenges to their long-held views of origins, sexuality, race, politics, social justice, and the like. The kinds of issues that are so explosive that we do everything we can to avoid them, or if we dare bring them up, we risk losing half the church. We thought we could help them do better if we drew on the basic confessions and practices of faith. Our goal was to engage conflict as an act of worship and as a practice of Christian discipleship. We wanted to recover modes of worship and faith practices that could help us engage conflict in ways that deepen love of God and neighbor.

Audacious, crazy, even arrogant? Of course, but why not? Why not audaciously trust our faith in God rather than just another political ideology? And we really weren't re-inventing the wheel, but initially trying to apply the pioneering work of American theologian Stanley Hauerwas and Scottish-American philosopher Alasdair MacIntyre to the conflicts church leaders were experiencing. We started gathering people who disagreed with each other over some of these "wicked problems" and told them we were going to worship and follow the structure of a common liturgy—to wrap the argument in the Gospel and then ask ourselves at the end whether the Spirit had produced fruit.

If it did, then our love of God and neighbor is richer and deeper. And if not, then what would we need to repent of, lament, and confess before trying it again because we honestly believe the Gospel gives us all we need to handle our serious conflicts with grace, even love.

That's really it in a nutshell—one of those simple but not easy propositions where we believe that the conflicts in a culture are precisely the places where Christians ought to be, and that the energy around these conflicts can be harnessed for discipleship.

To be honest, I came into the organization as a failure. I failed to lead the church I pastored through various conflicts that I presumed we could think and theologize our way out of, but we failed. Worse yet, the harder we tried, the worse we hurt each other. Yet I took the position at The Colossian Forum because my failure taught me an important truth: the church will not solve its disagreements on intellect and theology alone. We keep trying, but it's not working. Churches borrow from the wider culture. We've been formed by the same seeds. The problem is that the church is mimicking a divisive culture while proclaiming the Prince of Peace. This isn't the whole story, of course. There are lots of good, faithful people in all our churches, liberal and conservative, and sometimes they get it right. But for the most part, the church's reputation in this area is no different than that of the wider culture – win at all costs, no matter how ugly. This is the brand that the church currently has. The danger in this doomed approach to conflict is the eventual decline of the church in the West. I met once with a group of younger Christians and just to get them talking, I asked them who their mentors were.

"We don't have any," one responded. "We don't have those relationships."

I followed up by asking them what they thought of Jesus and his teachings.

"Oh, we're interested in Jesus," another answered. "But the church doesn't smell like Jesus."

What they were telling me was that the church just smells like the rest of the culture. There's this gap between the Jesus proclaimed and the political ideology that's twisted it.

We have this enormous population of younger Christians that is becoming spiritually homeless because they've seen Christianity lumped in with either Republican (evangelical) or Democrat (mainline) ideologies and want something more than affiliation with a political party. Or to put it another way, they don't need church if all church gives them is a theologized version of what they can get on FOX or CNN. I think they want much more from church, and when they don't get it, they leave. Or become nones.

In what is likely a sincere attempt to find a better way to handle these difficult issues, many churches choose another approach, and that's to ignore them. To pretend disagreements don't exist by never talking about them. This veneer of unity may be even more damaging because it requires a certain level of silent hypocrisy. As psychologist Adam Grant likes to say, "The absence of conflict isn't harmony, it's apathy." The person you sit next to on Sunday has a son who is gay and is looking forward to attending his wedding to another man. You believe same sex marriage violates God's design. But the two of you have no opportunity to talk about this, no language to speak of your deeply held beliefs, so you are forced to act as if it doesn't matter enough to bring it into the church you both love.

We don't want to see Christians of any age become so disillusioned with the church that they either leave or pretend, so we intentionally bring people together who disagree about really important issues and help them experience a better way to address those issues. Does it work? Not always, especially initially. But if all parties practice self-giving love for God and for neighbor, pursuing the Spirit, and returning to these guiding principles whenever they come to one of those places where things break down, amazing things happen. In fact, I have been overwhelmed by the gratitude people express at being given a space where left and right could be together for something greater than left or right.

What we offer is really basic Christian discipleship.

We're doing nothing new. We're gathering in the name of Jesus; that's our primary allegiance. We confess to each other that all things hold together in Christ, not because of something we did, but because of something that has already been done, and we get to participate in that. To do that well, we know that we have to pray. We have to meditate on the Scriptures, together, across our differences. We need to demonstrate our respect for each other by telling the truth—even truths that might initially hurt. And then we come together before God and see how we did.

One of those occasions occurred when we brought two preeminent scientists together who represented two sides of the origins debate that has divided churches, Christian schools and colleges, even families—all within the evangelical wing of the Christian church. Todd Wood is a young-earth creationist with a Ph.D. and post-doctoral work from the University of Virginia. Darrell Falk is an evolutionist with a similar academic pedigree. As part of a funded-project, over a period of three years, we asked them to meet with us or sometimes in front of audiences, and then instructed them to go after each other's views of origins, but within the framework of what we call The Colossian Way. Like most good church folk, they began by being really polite, and if they addressed their differences, they more or less danced around the edges.

Then one day, Darrell in uncharacteristic exasperation went for the throat, challenging Todd's scientific credentials, implying rather directly that he wasn't a real scientist. It clearly offended Todd, and Darrell knew it and instantly regretted it. I remember thinking to myself, "If the Holy

136

Spirit doesn't show up, we're screwed." And that's when they returned to the Gospel they both believed and loved. There was humility, tears, forgiveness, and ultimately joy. From that point on, they were able to directly, even aggressively challenge each other, but now with a language and a process that always ended in worship, prayer for each other, and praise. They never convinced each other of their "wrongness," but that was no longer their primary goal. Rather, two men who began as enemies—even enemies of the faith—became friends, brothers in Christ, whose lives modelled the reconciling power of Christ even while they disagreed about scripture.

This is The Colossian Way. It's coming together to worship, to be honest and be willing to get it wrong together. As Stanley Hauerwas said, "We worship a God that forgives, so we can tell the truth about our lives."

We can get it wrong. We can tell the truth about when we get it wrong because when we do, we can confess our sins and God is glorified. People have forgotten this, or if they remember it, it's only an idea; they haven't experienced it in the heat of a deep disagreement. They forget it the moment they walk into a conflict. We simply remind people of that Gospel, and when they taste it, they light up in wonder and amazement.

A few years ago, we met a man who grew up as a missionary kid and knew early on that he was gay. But because of his family's conservative faith, he remained in the closet. When he came out, he fell into a not uncommon cycle of despair and depression, even considering suicide. In perhaps an act of providence, he decided to check out a new church in his city, and the love and kindness he experienced there led him to return to his Christian faith. But soon this new church knew it needed to decide where it stood on the issue of same-sex relationships, including marriage. He watched and participated in the agonizing yet God-honoring process of decision making, and what stood out to him was the way everyone trusted God's Spirit to be present and guide their discussions. "I felt deeply loved throughout the process, but I also felt that I was called to love as well, and that this was a safe place for me—a place where I could follow and serve God."

When the consensus landed on the more traditional view of sexuality, he chose to remain with the church and take a vow of celibacy, even becoming one of its pastors. At one point, this man's mentor approached him and said, "I really don't know what I think of homosexuality, but I wonder if it isn't God's gift to you. But what I do know is that you are God's gift to us."

Not everyone will agree with this man's decision; he questions it himself often enough. But perhaps the bigger point is that this little church trusted the Gospel to walk them through a decision-making process that usually creates a bitter split between Christians who are convinced they are right and often use the Bible and theology as weapons. Our goal is not to worry much about who's right and who's wrong, but to invite the Holy Spirit to show up and see what happens.

When I started this organization, I was a systematic theologian not sure of what I was doing, and now I am a fervent evangelist for the work of the Spirit. Because when we gather together in the name of Jesus to look at those things that deeply divide us—when we get together face-to-face instead of on Facebook—we get to see and experience the Holy Spirit do new things in our midst, right before our eyes, over and over. By the power of the Spirit, our differences become occasions for grace and truth to burst forth.

Michael Gulker is the president of The Colossian Forum, based in Grand Rapids, Michigan. An ordained Mennonite minister, he holds an M.Div. from Duke University Divinity School. Before helping form The Colossian Forum, Michael served as pastor of Christ Community Church in Des Moines, Iowa. Learn more about Michael: colossianforum.org/about-us/team/

«21»

FORMING PEACEMAKERS, TRANSFORMING CONFLICT

Todd Deatherage

The conversation took place in one of those New Orleans restaurants with a famous chef, a storied past, and an overly attentive staff. John lived in the 9th Ward and drove tourists around the city for a living. He'd dropped many groups at this legendary establishment before, but he'd never been invited inside. After a couple days with our delegation of white Christian leaders from an Arizona church, and over a superlative three-course meal, he felt comfortable enough to tell us a little of his story, which involved a daughter who filled his heart with joy and pride, a near-death horror story about Hurricane Katrina involving a helicopter rescue, and a lot of bad experiences with the police. Across the table from him sat Mike, leaning in and listening intently. Mostly holding his own story in reserve, Mike gently asked questions that led nowhere except toward the heart of what John was trying to say. Mike is a church elder and a police captain. He'd come with his pastor and other congregational leaders on a Telos trip to the South to learn a more honest American story and to see the ongoing effects of systems of racism and injustice. He came as a listener and a learner, and he went home a changed

man. Among other experiences Mike had, John's willingness to speak candidly and share his lived experience with
a group of strangers who might be nothing more than a
bunch of do-gooders or "white saviors" opened eyes and
hearts.

On that night and for the rest of our journey, whenever things got uncomfortable, Mike chose not to dismiss
or defend, but to listen, to absorb what he heard, and to
self-interrogate. Being seen and heard on his own terms,
something opened up in John, too. At the end of the week,
he confessed surprise and some confusion about a group of
white Christians seeking to actually understand the rigged
system that shaped his life and the lives of people of color
in America. Mike took these stories home to Phoenix and
began to dream of how he might bring others on this journey. He's now organizing for law enforcement officers an
experience like the one he had as a way to begin to bridge
our divides, dismantle broken systems, and create new cultures that promote the flourishing of all.

John and Mike want peace, as do most of us. We want
to live in societies that are just and fair, in safety, with honored dignity, and where we and those we love can flourish.
Although Telos works with a variety of communities, much
of our work is with Christians who believe this kind of mutual flourishing was God's original design for us, present
in Creation, and expressed in the ancient Hebrew word
shalom. The wholeness, unity, and justice of Creation was
shattered in the Fall, but Jesus came to turn upside down
that broken order, to heal the sick, liberate the captives, and
give justice to the poor. In the Kingdom of God, *shalom* is

restored. Jesus both announced that this kingdom has now come, even though not fully, and he invites all who would follow him to be his ambassadors of reconciliation, to be peacemakers.

Our favorite definition of peacemaking is this simple one: collaboration across lines of difference for the common good. It presumes that while conflict is inevitable, disagreement and difference can help guide us to a world in which we can all flourish. At Telos, we work with Christians and non-Christians alike to form communities of American peacemakers to bring healing to seemingly intractable conflicts at home and aboard.

We invite Americans on unique journeys to the modern Holy Land to spend time with Palestinians and Israelis, getting to know them, their stories and the contexts of their lives. We visit the West Bank, meeting with Muslims and Christians, business leaders, nonviolence activists, and refugees, and we learn about the status of Palestinian citizens of Israel. We share a Shabbat meal with Orthodox Jewish families, visit the memorial to the Holocaust, meet with Israeli human rights activists, political leaders, security experts, and settlers. And we draw our chairs up extra close at the tables of those doing the work of coexistence, reconciliation, justice, and conflict resolution.

Telos also leads Americans into a deeper understanding of our own story with an experience in the U.S. South. These trips – which begin in New Orleans and the bayous of Louisiana and culminate in Selma and Montgomery, Alabama – widen the aperture on who we are as a people. These experiences equip us to engage and reimagine our complex history and the ongoing legacy of racial injustice and inequity.

Our approach offers insights into the role of power dynamics and inequality in conflicts, the connection between peace and justice, and the limits of violence to achieve any good ends. It shows us that the only way we ever move beyond an issue of historic injustice is by honestly addressing it. And it creates awareness of our own biases, complicity, and of our responsibility to act.

This kind of travel is deeply transformative. It was my own such life-changing experience while serving as a political appointee at the State Department in the Administration of President George W. Bush that led me from my evangelical and conservative background to cross my own line of difference and co-found Telos with a progressive, Yale-educated Palestinian-American attorney from California named Greg Khalil.

Following the immersive experiences we provide, Telos equips communities to act and advocate. We've seen pastors and leaders and their communities reorient themselves toward approaches to the Israeli-Palestinian conflict and racial justice in America grounded in this notion of mutual flourishing. The artists, musicians, and authors in our network are telling truer stories, singing better songs. Replicating and scaling this work across our country and our globe is not only how we heal our divides, but how we learn to allow our differences to drive flourishing for all.

Becoming the peacemakers the world needs often begins by going places you're not supposed to go, meeting people you're not supposed to meet, and opening yourself up to unusual conversations, relationships, and experiences. It then requires a commensurate willingness to work for systemic, social, political, and cultural change. This is not the unserious peacemaking of rainbows and unicorns, but the challenging work that opens the possibility for transformation. As Henri Nouwen said, "Every time in history that men and women have been able to respond to the events of their world as an occasion to change their hearts, an inexhaustible source of generosity and new life has been opened, offering hope far beyond the limits of human prediction."

There is no requirement, however, that you take an organized trip to immerse yourself in the lived reality of others. You can do that through honest relationships in your own communities, particularly with your neighbors who live on the margins, often victimized and unheard.

We can all be peacemakers – from teachers to diplomats, artists to politicians, stay-at-home parents to entrepreneurs, students to police officers, liberals to conservatives, activists to faith leaders. All who understand that we cannot deny our neighbor what we want for ourselves, who choose to live into a story bigger than our own, can be agents of healing and repair.

At Telos, we've distilled more than a dozen years of learning into what we call the Principles & Practices of Peacemaking, an articulation of the conceptual and moral foundations of honest peacemaking.

Following are six principles that undergird healthy approaches to addressing seemingly intractable interpersonal and international conflict. They can guide us to a better place on issues as varied as war, human and civil rights, oppression, the environment, local and global security, human migration, and inequality:

Principe One
Growth: Change is always possible

Human hearts, as well as cultures and systems of power, can change. Each of us impacts our reality. It's not a question of whether we change our world, but how. So we live and act in hope, striving for positive change in ourselves and for others.

Principle Two
Equity: True equality is actively won

All humans are created equal. Yet realizing true equality requires making opportunity and ownership accessible to all. Peacemakers honor the inherent dignity of all by actively building more equitable communities and societies. We reject social hierarchies, caste systems and false either/or binaries. There is no "us v. them," only "us, together." In the words of Mother Teresa, "We belong to each other."

Principle Three
Justice: Peace and justice are intertwined

As Dr. Martin Luther King made clear, "True peace is not the absence of tension: it is the presence of justice." Working for peace without justice is unserious, empty, and dangerous. Working for justice without concern for healing and reconciliation can degenerate into violence and revenge.

Principle Four
Relationship: Authentic relationships across lines of difference fuel transformation

Right relationship is the core of peacemaking. Intentionally cultivating relationships across lines of difference provides space for individual transformation, nurtures empathy and humility, and emphasizes the humanity of those different from us. Diverse relationships ground our ideologies, theologies and politics in the dignity and lived experience of others. They open the possibility for personal, communal and systemic change.

Principle Five
Nonviolence: "Nonviolence is a way of life for courageous people"–Dr. Martin Luther King, Jr.

Active nonviolence promotes freedom and justice and is grounded in a spirit of love and hope. Creative and clear resistance against all forms of violence – direct, structural, and cultural – heals our world and paves the path to reconciliation. Radical peacemaking is a courageous, counter-cultural, and purpose-driven way of life.

Principle Six
Mutual Flourishing: The end goal, or *telos*, is mutual flourishing

Peacemaking is the dangerous, difficult, and joyous practice of channeling righteous anger and demands for justice into the inclusive work of healing, mutual flourishing, and reconciliation.

Grounded in these six principles, here are six practical things each of us can do:

Practice One
Listen to understand

Before we can hope to heal our world, we must first learn to see it as it actually is. "Love's first act is to listen," is the sage wisdom of theologian Paul Tillich. We listen to understand before seeking to be understood. We meet the other, and ourselves, where we are.

Practice Two
Hold competing truths in tension

Peacemaking recognizes that my story is not the only story. Engaging the truths and experiences of others, even when they do not reconcile with our own, doesn't undermine our legitimacy; it instead opens possibilities for a better future for all. The physicist Niels Bohr puts it this way: "The opposite of a fact is falsehood, but the opposite of one profound truth may very well be another profound truth."

Practice Three
Own our agency and responsibility

We own our duty to leave this world better than we entered it. We embrace discomfort and uncertainty, which often signify and catalyze growth. Yet we act with humility, recognizing that peacemaking isn't primarily about outcomes or egos. We're not here to be heroes, but servants. The Psalmist tells us to "Seek peace, and pursue it" (Psalm 34:14, NRSV).

Practice Four
Center the leadership of the marginalized

Being near – or proximate – to those most vulnerable and listening to community-based leaders are two essential foundations of effective, ethical movements. Those closest to a problem often hold the most significant insight. Similarly, those who pay the greatest price of unjust systems often develop unique perspectives on how to transform those systems. We honor their resilience and expertise by amplifying platforms for their voices and by following their leadership, not imposing our own. Yet we do not abdicate our own responsibility and unique ability to lead within our communities, institutions and among our peers.

Practice Five
Self-interrogate and advocate

Jesus told us to first take the beam out of our own eye so that we could see more clearly to help remove the sliver from the eye of our neighbor. Peacemaking is an internal and an external practice in which we identify our biases, question our assumptions, challenge our own community, and leverage our privilege. Self-interrogation grounds our activism and advocacy in an integrity that better allows us to expose and challenge external systemic injustice and more effectively work across lines of difference.

Practice Six
Strive for "Beloved Community"

The *telos* of the peacemaker is not the defeat of "enemies," but the personal and systemic transformation that allows for mutual flourishing, reconciliation, and the creation of the "beloved community." We form communities that in composition and practice model the world we strive towards. Joyous, intentional, reflective, action-oriented communities replace unjust systems with just peace.

Todd Deatherage is Executive Director and Co-Founder of Telos. Prior to Telos, Todd spent sixteen years in senior positions in the legislative and executive branches of the U.S. government. Learn more about Todd: linkedin.com/in/todd-deatherage-3182448/

Learn more about Telos: howtohealourdivides.com/telos/

HEAD, HEART, HANDS

A Holistic Response to the Harms
of Social Divisions

Amy Julia Becker

When I set out to write a memoir about my participation in perpetuating social divisions and injustices, I resisted offering action steps. Part of that resistance arose from concern that such steps would become a checklist preventing readers from deep engagement with the ongoing problems of inequity in our nation. But part of my resistance arose from my own hesitation to confront my peers. I saw *White Picket Fences* as a gentle invitation to readers like me—white, affluent, educated Americans who were concerned about social divisions. I suspected that those same readers were also somewhat alarmed by the thought of political activism or calling out injustice. I didn't want a checklist. I didn't want to rock the boat. And I also felt inadequate. How could one person make any meaningful difference in the face of hundreds of years of oppression?

White Picket Fences: Turning Toward Love in a World Divided by Privilege was published in the fall of 2018. In it, I wrote about my concern about social divisions and my sense of paralysis in the face of the social forces around me.

I wrote about giving birth to a child with Down syndrome and recognizing that our daughter was both "inside" the walls of privilege and on the outside as well. I wrote about wrestling as a Christian to understand what it would look like to follow the words of Micah 6:8, to do justice, to love mercy, and to walk humbly with my God. I finished the book with a question, to myself as much as to the reader, an echo of Jesus' words to the paralytic by the pool of Bethesda: Do we want to get well?

As soon as *White Picket Fences* was released, I began travelling across the country and sharing stories with people from all over—rich and poor, white and Black and Asian American and Latinx, straight and gay, male and female. In those spaces, I found hundreds of people who related both to my sense of inadequacy and to my desire to engage in a meaningful way with healing the divisions in our nation. Almost everyone I talked to was ready to acknowledge the harm of our current situation. And they were longing to take small steps towards healing.

In response to these conversations, I began to formulate a simple way to engage with the historic harm of racism and injustice in our country. I wrote a short companion to White Picket Fences that explains a process of holistic response using our heads, hearts, and hands. The basic premise of *Head, Heart, Hands* is that in order to participate in healing social divisions we need to understand the problem (head), receive spiritual strength and nourishment (heart), connect with others (heart), and take meaningful ongoing action (hands), in whatever small, messy, local ways are available to us.

When it comes to taking action, there are three ways we can participate in healing social divisions. One, we can make individual changes. These manifest in the way we talk, how we gather information, how we spend and give money, and how we spend and give time. Two, we can use our influence to enact change. And three, we can work towards institutional change.

For me personally, individual changes began years ago, when we intentionally added chapter books with Black and brown characters to our kids' bookshelves. Those changes continued as we exposed our kids to news stories that we once thought were too violent or upsetting for them to view. We traveled as a family to the National Museum of African American History. Later, we took a longer journey to visit The Whitney Plantation—a former sugar plantation in Louisiana with tours from the perspective of enslaved people. We traveled to Montgomery and Birmingham to explore sites that marked our nation's history of lynching and commemorated the accomplishments of the Civil Rights movement.

These small decisions changed the way we talked about race and justice within our home. By the time George Floyd was murdered, our 9-year-old daughter understood something about the historical context of racism. I sat with her and showed her the photos of Derek Chauvin with his knee on Mr. Floyd's neck. I also showed her photos that honored Mr. Floyd as a church member, a father, and a brother. As a family, we participated in both a local demonstration and a local prayer gathering in response to that horrific scene and all it represents.

I'm not alone in taking small steps towards change, and I'm also not alone in looking for ways to participate in change on a larger influential and institutional level. Everyone has some level of local influence. This influence might extend to your neighborhood, town, faith community, school, or other civic groups. One area where I've been able to use my influence has been as a board member of a local arts organization. This organization has served a diverse group of students from towns and cities in our area over the years, but they had never formalized a commitment to connect the different communities. I was asked to pull together a group of diverse parents and community members from the different towns in order to consider how this organization could use education through the arts to connect kids from diverse backgrounds to one another in meaningful ways. We can only now imagine what these relationships and partnerships will lead to in the future, as the organization has committed to greater collaboration and connection in all aspects of its programming.

I've also been able to use my influence in our local church by choosing a curriculum* that introduced our students to themes of justice in the Bible. I've seen our pastor use her influence in gentle but persistent ways to challenge our small, rural, nearly-all-white congregation to engage with issues surrounding social division. First, she simply invited a fellow pastor who is a Black man to preach. From there, another pastor who is a Native American visited and then became a member of our church and eventual-

---

* *https://covchurch.org/justicejourney/*

ly a member of our pastoral staff. Our pastor also offered a small group study to read and talk through Jemar Tisby's *The Color of Compromise*. She has begun to mention news events from the pulpit—not in order to sway people's political leanings—but in order to offer prayer and compassion for our fellow Black and brown Christians who are more intimately connected to some of the tragic injustices throughout our nation. She has modeled small, gentle, but persistent and bold challenges to the status quo of our little congregation, and in so doing she has invited us all into a broader vision for the kingdom of God.

White men and women across the nation are starting to wake up to the history of injustice that has led to so many of our current divisions, and many of us are starting to take responsibility for undoing some of the harm. I spoke with one woman who lives on a working plantation that her family has owned since the 1920s. She wanted to think through whether they could transform their property into a place of peace instead of a symbol of historic oppression. She began by collaborating with local universities to research the history of the place in order to be able to name the harm perpetrated there. She connected with local Black citizens—including a descendant of one of the enslaved people from the plantation—in order to create a ceremony of repentance as well as to consider how this beautiful sprawling landscape could become a place of welcome and of healing.

Another woman reached out to me because her white children were zoned for a local public school that had almost no white students and almost entirely low-income students, but she could get priority status at a local magnet school with almost all white students. She learned the history of her local school system through a public radio podcast. She reached out to other parents in the neighborhood. She prayed about how to balance her kids' needs with her neighborhood's needs with her sense that God was calling her to participate in undoing the harm of years of functional school segregation. She entered the lottery system for her children's schooling and did not prioritize the "best" school in their local area, the school that has served primarily white students in recent years.

I've talked with employers who have only recently begun to insist that non-white applicants be considered whenever they are hiring, and executives who have stated that they will resign unless their boards of directors become more diverse. I've talked with Christians who have changed their charitable giving practices in order to support historically Black churches and ministries and non-profits with leadership from Black people and people of color. These are all examples of individuals making small but meaningful decisions to use their influence to address historic barriers to economic opportunity and access.

The final way that we can use our "hands" to effect change is on an institutional level. Institutions are conservative by nature. They think they need to remain consistent and predictable in order to flourish. And yet that same conservative stability can mean institutions become easily entrenched in historic injustices. The Civil Rights movement of the 1950s and 60s demonstrated most clearly both the complexity and possibility of institutional change. Institutional change depends upon individuals banding together in common cause. As individuals change their personal practices and look for ways to use their local influence to undo injustice, we become more connected to other local citizens and leaders who are willing to work towards institutional change.

The legacy of racism and other forms of discrimination in American society is far too great for any one of us to undo alone. But if we each use our head, heart, and hands to take the next small step, we can walk our way towards healing.

Amy Julia Becker is a writer and speaker on faith, family, disability, and privilege. She has written four books, and her writing has been published in USA Today, Christianity Today, The Washington Post and The New York Times. Learn more about Amy Julia: amyjuliabecker.com/

«23»

Just Show Up

How Food and Faith
Bring People Together

Mark Cryderman

As the pastor of a well-established suburban congregation in the Midwest, you could say that I had arrived. My wife enjoyed a rewarding job which helped supplement my already-adequate income. Our kids benefitted from a great school district. And we had purchased a lovely home on which I was beginning to use my carpentry skills to make some improvements. Although I was in my early forties and therefore not thinking much about retirement, I could see us staying there for the rest of my ministry. Except I couldn't shake a growing feeling that there was something more for us. I had no idea what that was, but even as our church prospered, I began to question if this was really where God wanted me to be.

The answer came with a fence.

One day my wife, Mary, and I agreed that we needed to build a fence around our backyard. We tried to decide just how high it should be and what type of fence would give us the privacy we wanted. From there it went to how we might fix up a little shed in our backyard. We spent quite a bit of time over the next few days talking about the fence, the shed, and other improvements we thought we needed, and it dawned on us almost simultaneously that all of our significant conversations lately had been about fixing up our house and property. Not about mission or ministry, but about the kind of fence we wanted, what color we would paint the shed, and other improvements around the place.

I distinctly remember saying to Mary at one point, "So this is it? We're done? The only thing we care deeply about is our house and yard?"

That was a turning point for us. We had to rethink what was going on—what was really important to us. At the same time, about ninety miles to the east of us in the Detroit suburb of Taylor, Michigan, our denomination—the Free Methodist Church—owned a building that was once a small Christian school but was unoccupied and piling up huge debt. So much so that our church and others in the denomination had been "taxed" to help pay the mortgage on the building, and the financial burden was serious enough for us that I had to lay off a couple of part-time staff. I remember thinking, "Instead of just paying for an empty building, wouldn't it be great if we could develop some kind of cool ministry there."

Be careful what you wish for.

We took the plunge. Sold our house. Moved into a small apartment. And with the help of some wonderful volunteers from area churches, created the Harbor—a safe place for the largely impoverished neighborhood surrounding us consisting of roughly one-third African-Americans, one-third Latinx, and one-third white people like Mary and me.

It became for us a blessed opportunity to learn how race and poverty play out in the real world. For example, when some in the area heard about our plans, they were not very encouraging: "Good luck trying to bring blacks, browns, and whites together. It will never work."

But it did, and I wish I could give you an elegant and strategic plan to explain how it worked, but the answer is simple, if not easy. During our time at the Harbor, we learned that one thing that brings people together is a common need. In the Detroit area, schools had suffered huge budget cuts, and typically when that happens, music and the arts are the first on the chopping block. So we developed an after-school program providing instruction in those areas. We also learned another important fact about education. The gaps between whites and African-Americans are at one level between September and June. But during the summer, whites travel, go to camp, visit libraries, go to the zoo, and enjoy all sorts of learning activities. Kids from impoverished families don't have those advantages and that's where the wheels come off in their educational progress. To counter that, we started a summer enrichment program with reading instruction, tutoring, and remedial work to help students from poor families keep up.

Toward the end of our first summer, we announced a big celebration—an art exhibit, complete with musical and dance performances, and the place was packed with white people, black people, and Latinx people shoulder-to shoulder. We eventually started a church of sorts—Sunday Brunch and Stories—and I was now the pastor of a multicultural church of people who never used to get along with each other, but because their children's needs were being met, they became friends. It may sound simplistic, but one of the best ways to heal division is to meet the common needs that all people share. People tend to get along if they all feel they're being treated equally.

It was an important lesson I took with me to my next assignment: Dinner Church.

Dinner Church is a nationwide movement that aims to serve people who are poor and oppressed by simply inviting them to a meal. If they want to, they can stay for a ten-minute story from the Bible, but we make it clear—first and foremost we're here to serve you dinner. A local Catholic parish let us use their community center, and Mary began preparing meals early Monday morning for the 5:30 dinner that night. From the beginning we wanted to serve a healthy, sumptuous meal on real tablecloths and make our new neighbors feel safe, accepted, and loved. We put up signs and posters in the neighborhood and then showed up (remember those words: showed up).

Once again, it worked, and we now had another church, albeit one that looks little like the suburban church where we might have served until we retired. The majority of our parishioners are black and among the poorest of the poor. Most lived in the same housing project and on the first night, we set up ten tables. The first ten people who came in each sat down at a separate table. I inquired of the manager of the project why they did that, and she quickly responded, "Oh they hate each other." However, once they actually sat down and shared a meal together, they began talking with each other. For the first few Mondays, they would leave when I did, but after that, I left a room full of new friends who refused to leave because they were having so much fun. They had lived in the same building for years and never got along. Food brought them together.

Knowing that we couldn't handle all the food preparation on our own, we solicited help from a mostly-white church who sent a few couples to lend a hand. What I learned from that was how fearful white Christians are of people of color. That first night they stood on one side of the table to serve the food, then sat by themselves to eat. Afterwards, I called them together and told them that from now on, they needed to go and sit with the people they served, get to know them, and more important, become vulnerable to our church folk. I could tell they were uneasy about it, but to their credit, the next Monday they did exactly that, and now many of those volunteers have developed genuine friendships with our Dinner Church attendees. One, a dear woman in her seventies, has become the unofficial grandma to the children who show up.

Did I enter this phase of my ministry trying to heal the racial and economic divides in America? No, but I had always believed that God is on the side of the poor and oppressed; however, like many evangelical suburban pastors, never really did much about it. I always had great respect for the way my little denomination had opposed slavery in the nineteenth century and historically had served the poor, but not until I left the comfort of my suburban pastorate had I really begun to understand how systemic racism and poverty affects generations of American citizens and more important, what can be done about it.

Have our efforts made a huge dent in the divisions within the city of Detroit? I'll answer that by telling you a story about Margaret, an elderly white woman who lives in a run-down, rat-infested house where the water is either turned off by the city or frozen in the winter. A hoarder with obvious mental-health issues, she's one of our regular attenders. When she shows up for church, her baggy pants often slip down her legs, revealing her naked backside. Whenever that happens, two black women who have very little themselves, quietly walk over next to her, pull up her pants, and give her a hug. It's a small act, but a huge one in our divided culture.

We are still neophytes when it comes to cross-cultural ministry, but here's what we've learned about bringing people together who think they do not like each other very much:

1. Show up. Literally. We left our apartment in Taylor to move to Detroit in order to be with those we intended to serve. We do not have all the answers and we've probably made a lot of mistakes. But we have learned that you will absolutely make zero progress if you don't show up where the needs are the greatest. Good things happen if you keep showing up.

2. Meet people at their point of greatest need. We might think that black people need to get along better with white people. I can guarantee you that oppressed minorities are more concerned about other things. For our Dinner Church, its things we've never had to worry about: (1) Will my kids have enough to eat? (2) Will they be safe? (3) Will we have a place to sleep tonight? Meet their needs, not yours.

3. Learn the beauty of humility in leadership. Oppressed minorities are quite accustomed to white people—and even more affluent black and brown people—showing up with all the answers; telling them what they need to do to get ahead and then driving back to the suburbs in their Mercedes. We learned early on to listen, not just out of politeness, but because those we desire to serve have much to teach us. My great friend and ministry assistant is a black man who was given hard drugs by his uncle when he was seven years old. When he speaks, I listen because he knows his people, their needs, their hopes. By listening, they are becoming we.

4. Trust the Gospel. Jesus has given us all we need to heal the racial and economic divides in our nation. He calls the poor "blessed" and stands with the oppressed. To the extent that we follow his example, we will see greater unity and healing.

When I first began having rumblings in my soul that ministry was more than owning a nice house and preaching every Sunday to people who looked like me, I began making excuses for why I wasn't the right person or this wasn't the right time to make a change. Had I listened to those excuses we would have missed out on what has become an unimaginable adventure of experiencing the beautiful diversity of the body of Christ. Great things happen when you just show up.

Mark and Mary Cryderman are a ministry couple affiliated with the Free Methodist Church of North America, serving in Detroit, Michigan. For more information about Dinner Church: howtohealourdivides.com/dinner-church-movement/

TOWARD A WORLD
BEYOND ENEMIES

Michael McRay

There was something in the way she moved. Smile wide across her face like it'd been drawn, shoulders pumping to the drumbeat, feet shuffling and stomping in rhythm. Her pink-embroidered top clung to her torso while her ocean blue skirt flung wildly as she spun. She twirled and clapped, calling out a song that the forty other women behind her in white plastic chairs echoed. The call and response of a group in sync with one another.

I was in Taba, Rwanda, dancing with the women of SEVOTA. It was January 2018, and I was accompanying a group of dance students from Texas Christian University as their Reconciliation Scholar. The women we were with in that old schoolhouse auditorium had been brutalized, bereaved, and burdened by the genocide of 1994. Three years after the killing ended, the mayor of Taba became the first Rwandan to stand trial for genocide. He not only allowed the murders of Tutsis in his village, but he gave the Hutu militia the names and addresses and oversaw many killings. His case also saw the first ever conviction of rape as a war crime. And this would not have happened without the women of Taba—*these* women of Taba.

After the horrors of 1994, many women did not and could not speak about what happened to them. The truth of what happened seemed to have become another casualty of the genocide. But then, Godelieve Mukasarasi—the woman I described above—began bringing the women of Taba together to tell their stories to each other. Eventually, three of these women, including Godelieve, traveled to Tanzania to testify to the crimes of their former mayor. He was convicted and sentenced to life in prison.

But Godelieve had the wisdom to know stories aren't just told with words, and healing can't just come from language; the stories and healing must also come from the body. So months after the genocide, she established SEVOTA—"Solidarity for Widows and Orphans for Work and Self-Promotion"*—which, among other things, uses dance as a way to rebuild the individual and community after genocide. The sexual assaults these women endured displaced them from their own bodies and dislocated their sense of security. Through the movement of dance, the women of Taba told me they are finding ways back into their own bodies. They are coming home to themselves.

After the dust in the room settled from the shuffles and kicks of all our dancing, one woman stepped forward to thank us for coming. But her thanks to us was rightly brief; instead, she thanked Godelieve. "Before Godelieve, life was pain and hardship. Now, we are alive again. We have peace and are happy."

---

*For more on SEVOTA, see
https://www.peaceinsight.org/en/organisations/sevota/

In the biblical book of Ezekiel, there is a story where a valley of dry bones is resurrected, with sinews and flesh and life and breath. That day in Taba, I saw that story alive.

———

In recent years, I have wandered the world, searching for stories that might save us from our divisions. So many societies have been diseased with the plague of violence and enmity, and I wanted to learn lessons from peacebuilders in places like Israel and Palestine, Northern Ireland, South Africa, and Rwanda.* What wisdom would they offer for the wounds of my home country of the United States? In each country I visited, I partnered with remarkable organizations, like SEVOTA, to gather the stories I sought, and I witnessed the varied and vital work these organizations do in their home places.

In Israel and Palestine, I soaked in the beauty of the Parents Circle. Membership to this organization requires having lost someone to the conflict. Israelis and Palestinians who have buried their children, parents, siblings, or other family members meet together in this organization. It's one of the only organizations in the world, they told me, that doesn't want new members.

Two of the members I met were Rami Elhanan and Bassam Aramin. Rami is an Israeli father whose own father survived Auschwitz but whose daughter did not survive 13. Smadar was killed in Jerusalem by a Palestinian sui-

———

*These stories, except for Rwanda, are featured in full in my 2020 publication *I Am Not Your Enemy*.

cide bomber. Bassam Aramin is a Palestinian father whose 10-year-old daughter Abir was returning from school when she was shot in the back of the head and killed by an Israeli soldier. The justification of violent conflict says these two men have every reason to hate one another. But they don't. Through the work of the Parents Circle, Rami and Bassam—and hundreds of other bereaved people—find common ground through their shared loss. They know what it is to grieve. They know what it is to learn that some dreams will never come to pass. And as Rami said to me, "If we who paid the highest price possible—if we can talk to each other, then anyone can. Anyone should."

Members of the Parents Circle speak to audiences around the world garnering support for their work, but they also take their message where it matters most: the youth of their own societies. The potential future combatants. Through their stories of burying their loved ones, they hope to shift mindsets. Rami said they want the children of their land to know: "This is not our destiny to keep on killing each other forever. We can change it. We can break, once and for all, the cycle of violence and revenge and retaliation. And the only way to do this is simply by talking to each other. It will not stop unless we talk."*

———

In Northern Ireland, there's a place of lumpy crossings. I know that doesn't make sense at the moment, but it will soon.

---

*For more on the Parents Circle, see *https://www.theparentscircle.org/*. For more on Rami and Bassam's stories, see chapter 10 in my book *I Am Not Your Enemy*.

On the north coast of County Antrim is a center called Corrymeela. It is the oldest peace and reconciliation community on the island of Ireland. During the Troubles that rocked Northern Ireland in the latter part of the 20th century, Corrymeela served as a refuge for people fleeing the violence. Today, it offers shelter for projects of difficult conversations. People who find it trying to sit in the same room with each other give it a try at Corrymeela. Over cups of tea and arguments over the possibilities of peace, they stumble through the rocky terrain of truth-telling, learning how to hold the tense truth of another alongside their own.

Corrymeela welcomes over ten thousand visitors per year, and their calendar of events addresses issues of sectarianism, marginalization, legacies of conflict, and public theology. It is a community committed to learning how to live well together, especially among difference. This is, after all, what reconciliation is about: learning to live together well.

Once, I asked my friend Pádraig Ó Tuama, the former leader of Corrymeela, what the name Corrymeela meant. He told me this story. Some time ago, people named the land, where this center now sits, *Corrymeela*. They thought it meant "hill of harmony" in Old Irish. A perfect name for a place of reconciliation: hill of harmony. Years later, though, someone arrived who truly knew Old Irish etymology and said, "Actually, *corrymeela* means something more like 'place of lumpy crossings.'" And all the people rejoiced. Because in their work for reconciliation, harmony had been rare. But "place of lumpy crossings" was a name that could hold them well.

There's a saying at Corrymeela: "Corrymeela begins when you leave." Corrymeela is not just a place; it's a practice. And there are Corrymeela member groups scattered across Ireland and beyond—communities of intention that meet together with affection and accountability to embrace the project of trying to live together well in a world that makes it difficult.* What a challenge for us all.

———

Here in the United States, I once witnessed storytelling transform a woman. I'll call her Kandice. She and some others had gathered for a Narrative 4 story exchange I was facilitating on the theme of immigration. In a story exchange, paired participants privately tell each other a true personal story, and then retell their partner's story to the whole group, using first-person pronouns, as if their partner's story were really their own.

Kandice—a black immigrant woman—had come to this event at a friend's invitation. The moment she walked through the door I could tell she did not want to be there. Her eyes screamed exhaustion and her body looked tense. I walked up to her, and said, "Welcome. I'm glad you are here. How are you feeling about all this?"

She answered, "I'm just going to warn you. I'm not in a good place today. I don't know what's going to come up for me during this, so you should just be ready."

I thanked her for her honesty and her courage to come

———

*For more, see _www.corrymeela.org_, as well as chapter six in my book _I Am Not Your Enemy._

with her friend to this strange gathering of strangers. "I want you to know that you can do whatever you need to for your own well-being. If you need to leave, please feel free to do that."

"No, I'll stay," she replied, her head still down. "Just don't expect much from me."

I ended up pairing Kandice with a US-born white woman named Natalie who was about her same age. Kandice's story was soaked in suffering—immigration from the Caribbean at a young age, foster care, abuse, hardship—and Natalie wept through the retelling. Kandice wept too. After we'd heard all the stories present, I transitioned the group into a debrief. When my eyes met Kandice's, she now looked as if she could float up from her chair and through the ceiling. When she spoke, she said, "I feel *physically lighter* after hearing Natalie tell my story, as if the weight of that story isn't just mine anymore; there's someone else to help carry it. And as I watched her struggle with the pain of my story, all I wanted to do was hold and comfort her. I've now realized that that's what I've never been able to do for myself."*

This is the power of the Narrative 4 story exchange. I've seen this story exchange methodology shorten the distance between people on opposite sides of the U.S. gun debate, people from different faith backgrounds, youth from varied economic backgrounds, people whose imaginations of each other had previously been populated by only stereotypes. Since 2012, Narrative 4 has facilitated the exchange

---

*A version of this story first appeared in my chapter, "On Parables," in Brittney Winn Lee's edited compilation, _Rally_.

of over 200,000 stories across 20 countries and half the U.S. states. They are building an expansive network of practitioners and ambassadors for their mission: to increase people's capacity to practice empathy, and then to turn that empathy into action.*

The world is seasoned generously with people and organizations doing all they might to build peace. My life has let me meet only a handful of these multitudes, and it's only taken a handful to teach me much about how to heal our divides.

They taught me that we heal our divides by telling the truth about those divides.

They taught me that we heal our divides by starting with the divisions within ourselves and our own bodies. Bridge-building starts on the shores, not in the middle of the water.

They taught me that we heal our divides through courage and humility and curiosity.

They taught me that we heal our divides through listening to the stories of others and to the stories those others tell about us.

They taught me that we heal our divides through patience, perseverance, and a commitment to save others from the pain we feel.

They taught me that we heal our divides through knowledge, yes, but more importantly through *acknowledgement.*

---

* For more, see *www.narrative4.com.*

And they taught me that we heal our divides by showing up, time and time again, to stumble through the place of lumpy crossings, in search of another way of living.

Michael McRay is an award-winning writer, consultant, facilitator, and story-practitioner. His work explores the capacity of narrative to make meaning, reduce harm, transform conflict, and reconcile relationships. Michael works with individuals, groups, and organizations around the world to find, craft, and tell their most meaningful stories. Learn more about Michael: michaelmcray.com/

«25»

PEACE CATALYST

Following Jesus, Waging Peace

Martin Brooks

Peace Catalyst International (PCI) is a Christian peace-building organization that started in 2010 to heal the divides between Evangelical Christians and Muslims. In time, we saw that the practices we used to bring Christians and Muslims together could also empower the church to help heal the divides of race, nationality, sex and gender, and politics.

We now have Christian peacebuilders in 17 cities and three countries, and we are looking for more people to join PCI as full-time peacebuilders, bi-vocational peacebuilders, or volunteers.

Our goal is shalom, not just the cessation of violence but also the restoration of the harmony that God declared to be "very good" in Genesis 1-2.

Our method is to prioritize the teachings and example of Jesus. We pursue peace by challenging, equipping, and inviting Christians to join their neighbors in pursuing shalom for all.

The Early Days of Peace Catalyst

PCI's strategy has always been to influence decision-makers while initiating grassroots peacebuilding. PCI began this work by organizing interfaith dialogue events. We believed that if we could expose people to better information and then get them in the same room to see for themselves that what we were saying was true, things would gradually improve. Imams and pastors answered questions in front of diverse audiences, but some conservative Christians were resistant. They based their objections to Muslims on fears of safety and then used theology to justify their boundaries. Dr. Rick Love, founder and president of PCI, wrote articles and recorded videos to provide counter-narratives. To influence national and international perspectives, PCI started *Evangelicals for Peace** at a conference we organized at Georgetown University. This grew into a collaborative working group of ten evangelical organizations that tried to help the church respond better to the foreign-born, both domestically and internationally. In 2015, Rick worked with the International Center for Religion and Diplomacy to bring Muslim and Christian leaders to Temple University to discuss religious freedom and islamophobia. Peace Catalyst has consistently worked with academics, governments, and religious leaders to shift the dominant narratives.

In 2016, PCI started a two-year multi-city project that required staff to pair with Muslim partners to receive training together, assess each city's situation, and create resil-

---

* *https://www.evangelicalsforpeace.org/*

174

iency plans. When we completed the project, we saw even more clearly how collaboration had strengthened the bond between partners and dramatically improved our work's effectiveness. Although collaboration had always been important in PCI's work, we began to name "collaboration" as a guiding principle for future PCI projects. After ten years of mending divides, PCI peacebuilders have learned to follow the path of understanding, connecting, collaborating, and celebrating.

Understanding

The Bible says we should be quick to hear, slow to speak, and slow to anger (see James 1:19). Understanding the perspective of the other is a critical first step toward healing. It requires humility and holding our presuppositions and initial conclusions loosely. We often do not understand and therefore prescribe the wrong remedies simply because we have not taken the time to reflect.

Peter and Liz Digitale Anderson launched a new Peace Catalyst site in Minneapolis in 2019. They spent a year networking, reading, and making scouting trips before moving to Minneapolis. They shared meals and coffee with neighbors, activists, and leaders, listening to their stories. They showed up for locally organized events to discover what needs were most relevant and which resources were readily available. Through this ongoing posture of understanding, presence, and humility, Peter and Liz continue to find new ways to join in with their neighborhood's collective transformation.

Peace Catalyst continually seeks to increase understanding by collecting, writing, and distributing articles through our webpage and social media to help people understand each other and the times in which we live. PCI started a free online community on Facebook called the Christian Peacebuilding Network to help peacebuilders connect and learn peace theology and peacebuilding skills. We have also released our first podcast series, which features Muslim women peacebuilders. On a grassroots level, staff in Seattle, Los Angeles, Boise, Milwaukee, Raleigh, Louisville, Sarajevo, and many other places offer introductory training for Christians who are interested in getting involved in peacebuilding work. All of these are attempts to help build understanding and catalyze Christians into the broader peacebuilding movement.

Connecting

In 2018, PCI organized a monthly gathering of imams, rabbis, Catholic priests, and protestant ministers in Louisville, KY. These leaders wanted to keep the group small and intimate. One protestant minister said, "I need you as friends in my life so I can call when I have questions. I do not want to misrepresent or unintentionally spread lies about your faith traditions." Anyone can read a book about another group, but peacebuilding is relational. Peacebuilders must do more than read articles and listen to news reporters. They need to meet and talk to the other.

The value of these relational investments is not always apparent, but they create a strong social fabric that becomes essential in times of conflict. When a televangelist in Florida blamed Jewish people for undermining President Trump and called for the deportation of Jewish people from the United States, it frightened one of these rabbis. She reached out to this group to determine the reach of this televangelist and to seek reassurance. Several in the group offered their homes as a safe refuge if things should ever escalate. How can we follow the commands to "seek peace and pursue it" (Ps 34:14, 1 Pet 3:11 NRSV) if we refuse to invest in relationships?

When Becca Pugh graduated from American University with a graduate degree in peacebuilding, she wanted to integrate her secular education with her faith. Becca became a PCI representative in Washington, DC. Hurunnessa Fariad also lived in DC and had helped lead some PCI programs. Hurunnessa serves as the Director of Outreach and Interfaith at the All Dulles Area Muslim Society Center and leads the only mosque-based youth choir in the United States. Over many lunches, Becca and Hurunnessa talked about life, work, and everything in between. They attended the National Prayer Breakfast and sat together at the Middle East Prayer Breakfast. They now plan events together and share many friends in common. This is more than a professional working relationship; this is a true friendship. Becca connects her church in DC to her peacebuilding work by inviting her friends into these new relationships. As Becca and Hurunnessa demonstrate, connections must become more than being in the same room. Collaboration is critical for successful peacebuilding.

Collaborating

To say you have friends in an out-group is fine, but collaboration can be a problematic next step. PCI has found the best way to collaborate across lines of division is by identifying shared values and collaborating for a common goal. For example, if divergent groups agree that all people have inherent value or that justice for all is essential, they can collaborate to meet these goals. If, on the other hand, we try to fix the problems we see with someone's worldview as a precondition of working together, collaboration becomes virtually impossible. Jesus said that the most important things we could do were to love God and love others (see Mark 12:29-31). Relationships with people must be more important to the peacebuilder than insisting on ideological purity.

Bryan and Stephanie Carey were engineers who had hearts for peacebuilding. After returning to school and completing their Masters of Divinity, concentrating on "Justice, Peacebuilding, and Conflict Transformation," they chose to work with Peace Catalyst in Sarajevo, Bosnia and Herzegovina. Bryan and Stephanie embraced this collaborative approach. As they learned the language and settled their young family in a new city, they also fixed printers and rebuilt websites for their new Bosnian friends. They translated articles into English as volunteers for local peacebuilding organizations. They did their best to amplify the voices and perspectives of local peacebuilders.

Trust between the Careys and local peacebuilders increased as an awareness of each partners' strengths and capacities grew. When Christian groups expressed interest in visiting Bosnia to support the work, Bryan and Stephanie asked their local friends whether such a visit could genuinely support local peacebuilding efforts. The Careys and their Bosnian collaborators co-designed a learning pilgrimage in which visitors from the States could come learn from all sides of the war. This was not westerners coming to "fix Bosnia"; Bosnians were the teachers, sharing their story and their wisdom. As participants recounted and listened to the painful memories of war, parallels emerged between Bosnia's conflicts and the widening social divisions developing in the States. This collaboration allowed for a powerful shared experience, uniting hearts from opposite sides of the world.

This is peacebuilding. We understand, we connect, and we collaborate to take small steps toward shalom, the mutual thriving of all.

Celebrating

In *The Moral Imagination*, John Paul Lederach says people have to imagine themselves being in a relationship with another group before they can realize that vision. Stories allow people to see what has happened in other contexts and to imagine new possibilities for themselves.

In 2015, vandals sprayed hateful graffiti on a mosque in Louisville. The imam and PCI staff had collaborated on many projects. The day after the vandalism, Mayor Fischer challenged the city to be compassionate. "This does not represent who we are," Fischer told the community. The next day, around 1,000 people from Louisville came to the mosque to paint over the graffiti and clean up. One Pakistani member of the mosque then wrote an op-ed* that appeared in Pakistan's largest English newspaper. He told this story and asked if Pakistan was willing to do the same for religious minorities there. Because of Louisville's response to this vandalism, PCI's Pakistani friend was able to cast a vision of Muslims and Christians living in peace. Through telling his story, he dismantled stereotypes of Americans and advocated for religious freedom in Pakistan. PCI has written elsewhere about the ripple effects† of our collaborative work.

Join Us

Peace Catalyst exists to catalyze Christian involvement in collaborative peacebuilding work with our neighbors for the flourishing of all. Think of us as a sending agency for Christian peacebuilders. We are working to shift the Christian narratives about the nature of God's mission and the Church's vocation. We're recruiting and equipping grassroots peacemakers and scaling up their collective contributions to shalom by connecting them to an international network of peacebuilders. We are building an organization of volunteers and part-time and full-time staff to follow Jesus and wage peace either where they are or on the other side of the world.

Are you ready to be a peace catalyst with us and pursue shalom for all? Reach out to us at *www.peacecatalyst.org*.

---

https://tribune.com.pk/story/961566/would-we-have-done-any-better
†*https://www.peacecatalyst.org/blog/2020/3/10/ripple-effects*

WAYS YOU CAN GET INVOLVED

Martin Brooks is Interim President of Peace Catalyst International, and has been with the organization since 2011. Martin has a Masters of International Relations from Near East University and is pursuing a Doctorate of Education and Social Change at Bellarmine University. Learn more about Martin Brooks:
peacecatalyst.org/martinbrooksbio

Learn more about Peace Catalyst International:
howtohealourdivides.com/peace-catalyst-international/

CROSSING BOUNDARIES
OF FAITH

Wes Granberg-Michaelson

If we cannot have true friendship across boundaries, Jesus is a liar." So said Dr. Dana Robert when she addressed the International Committee of the Global Christian Forum. Professor Robert is one of the leading experts on the history and practice of Christian mission, teaching at Boston University's School of Theology. Her most recent book is *Faithful Friendship: Embracing Diversity in Christian Community*. In her sharing with the Global Christian Forum, Robert catalogued through powerful historical examples how relationships that overcame formidable boundaries of race, culture, class, and nationality were pivotal in strategic moments of Christian mission throughout the world.

Robert's words were welcomed by the 25 members of the committee, meeting virtually from all points of the world, which guides the work of the Global Christian Forum. For over two decades, this pioneering ecumenical initiative work has been guided by practices which build friendship and trust across sharp divisions in world Christianity. Those divisions, nurtured over centuries, have bred hostility, judgment, rejection, and even violence between those of a faith whose founder commanded them to love one another.

Christians around the world are not one big happy family. They are divided into various "families" who often regard one another as heretical and outside of the "true faith." Such divisions do not have merely cultural and social consequences. Many who hold them believe they have eternal consequences. So, the stakes are high. In global terms, four primary families comprise those who identify as Christian, accounting for one-third of the world's population:

The Catholic Church

Nearly one-half of all the world's Christians belong to the Catholic family, with a structure of authority ultimately accountable to the Pope and the Vatican. While ecumenical understandings have advanced since Vatican II, Catholics still consider themselves as the truest expression of the one Body of Christ.

The Orthodox Church(es)

Like the Catholic Church, the Orthodox Churches trace their roots directly to the Apostles. But in 1054, a major, definitive and hostile break, called the Great Schism, took place between the two, centered in Rome and Constantinople, with each side declaring the other as heretical, and excommunicating themselves from one another. Despite goodwill gestures toward reconciliation, that formal rift remains.

Historic, Protestant Churches

The Reformation, beginning in central Europe, established new "Protestant" churches breaking with the existing "Catholic" church. Religious wars ensued, complicated by political ambitions, in which millions died. Protestants endlessly divided themselves from one another resulting in thousands of separate denominations, many of which remain officially divided and not in communion with one another.

Pentecostals and Evangelicals

The "newest" churches in the world, with large majorities in the Global South, are from this emerging family. For Pentecostals, growth has been astonishing, now accounting for one out of four Christians in the world. Most evangelicals and Pentecostals live in closely bounded religious and cultural bubbles, regarding those from Christianity's other three families as unfaithful, and even in need of eternal salvation.

In the last century, ecumenical initiatives have attempted to address these formidable, crippling divisions in the church. Advances are notable, yet serious and nearly insurmountable divisions persist. In broad terms, the World Council of Churches, the most dramatic expression of the ecumenical movement, has brought together many churches from the Historic Protestant family and the Orthodox family. The Catholic Church, while cooperating with some programs, has remained outside its membership. And most Pentecostal and evangelical churches have ignored or condemned official expressions of the ecumenical movement.

Faced with these persistent barriers of faith, with high mistrust, stereotypes, and judgments solidifying entrenched divisions, an innovative approach to building Christian unity was needed. Off-the-record meetings of a few willing leaders from each of these four families were convened, beginning in 1998. A proposal to create a new safe space called the "Global Christian Forum" gradually emerged through four years of quiet dialogue.

A key challenge, however, was how to build trust and relationship between Christian leaders whose traditions and constituencies were completely divided from one another in mutual recrimination and had been for centuries. At one of the first gatherings, Dr. Cecil "Mel" Robeck, a noted Pentecostal theologian and a courageous, lonely pioneer in ecumenical dialogue, suggested that those present begin by simply sharing their personal stories or testimonies of their faith journey.

The result was remarkable, as an entirely different and powerful starting point. Normally, ecumenical meetings and programs would focus in one of three ways. 1) Dialogue around theological differences searching for points of convergence and agreement; 2) Cooperation around common challenges in society and the world, such as migration, climate change, health, etc.; or 3) Dialogue and potential cooperation around engagement in God's mission and evangelism. All have their place. But the deepest barriers were not being crossed.

When people began, in a small group, taking the time to tell the story of their journey with Jesus Christ, or to share how God had brought them through life's journey to their present place of ministry, the dynamic of the group shifted. Stereotypes and judgments were disarmed. Assumptions about those in other factions of Christianity were over-turned. A climate for trust and dialogue began to emerge.

This became the methodology of the Global Christian Forum. Every gathering would begin with the sharing of faith stories from each participant. All the time necessary to do so was taken. The point was not to find agreement. Rather, it was to create a space and climate which engendered trust. Then, discussion of issues or challenges needing attention could begin without the deep suspicion and quiet hostility that otherwise might reign.

The work of the Global Christian Forum, with the foundation of this methodology, emerged. Regional consultations of church leaders from across the spectrum of theology and tradition were held in Africa, Asia, Latin America, and Europe. This led to the first global gathering, held in Limuru, Kenya in November 2007.

One personal story demonstrates how space for sharing faith stories transforms relationships and builds new ecumenical space. The late Dr. James Leggett was Presiding Bishop of the International Pentecostal Holiness Church, and Chairman of the Pentecostal World Conference. We had become friends through our involvement in Christian Churches Together. As a major global Pentecostal leader, I wanted Jim to come to the Global Christian Forum's gathering in Limuru. He was reluctant, concerned about attitudes and possible criticism of some in the Pentecostal community. But he agreed.

When we met the first evening at the conference center in Limuru, Dr. Leggett asked me hesitantly, "Do you think that the General Secretary of the World Council of

Churches would be willing to meet with me?" I assured him that Sam Kobia would be delighted to do so. Over lunch the next day, Dr. Leggett discovered that Sam Kobia's father was a Pentecostal minister. The dialogue that followed, based on their personal narratives, established trust between the leaders of two global Christian organizations that rarely had any relationship with one another.

With about 240 leaders of all the Christian "families" from around the world, the Limuru gathering began by dividing the participants into small groups where each person shared his or her faith story. That took much of the first day. And the result was spiritually and relationally electric.

A profound sense of belonging to one another, transcending entrenched divisions and stereotypes, was created when an Anglican Bishop from Canada, whom Christ called into ministry when she was a teenager, shared her vision with a Pentecostal leader from Ghana, who was called unexpectedly into the church, and then an Orthodox bishop from Syria shared his dramatic spiritual journey. These became mystical moments crystallizing the truth of sharing one faith, one Lord, and one baptism.

The gathering then moved into sharing emerging realities in the churches from various regions and exploring the common challenges of God's mission in the world. Vision and energy flourished. By the conclusion, those gathered strongly affirmed the value of this unique time, and the imperative need for this initiative to continue. When a final draft communique was shared, it was met not with debate, but with the spontaneous singing of the Doxology.

Observers called the gathering in Limuru, Kenya "a

watershed in Christian history." It marked a breakthrough ecumenically. Barriers of faith were crossed by creating a safe space for participants to share their stories. At the conclusion, James Leggett came up to me to say that these days in Limuru had forever changed his understanding of the broader body of Christ around the world. Until his death, Dr. Leggett became a courageous Pentecostal voice for building Christian unity.

In the years since then, the work of the Global Christian Forum has gone forward, always undergirded by the practice of beginning with time and space for each participant to share the personal story of his or her faith journey. In 2011, another global gathering was held in Manado, Indonesia. At its closing worship service, five participants from different regions and traditions who were experiencing the Global Christian Forum for the first time shared in the sermon. They each spoke of the joy, and often the surprise, in what they discovered – some of them interacting with those from Christian traditions that they barely knew even existed. The unity of heart and Spirit they experienced had a profound effect, shared by most all the participants from 65 different countries.

The same dynamic overflowed at the third global gathering, held in Bogota, Columbia in 2018. The Global Christian Forum's methodology remains key. I remember, in my sharing group, the Anglican ecumenical officer who was a math student and suddenly had a vision in the middle of a class which took him into ministry. A high official from the Vatican shared the pain of how his church judged others when he grew up in Ireland. A Pentecostal pastor from

Asia, formerly a businessman dramatically called into ministry, listened intently to those whom previously he would judge, and could never imagine sharing in prayer together. Those stories multiplied, with their effects rippling through the plenary sessions which followed.

When Professor Dana Robert met with the International Committee of the Global Christian Forum in 2021, we were looking beyond Covid-19, and beginning to plan our fourth global gathering. We have experienced the truth of what Dr. Robert shared. "If we cannot have true friendship across boundaries, Jesus is a liar." We have discovered over the last two decades that crossing the formidable and fearsome boundaries of tradition, history, theology, race, and culture within world Christianity can begin by listening to each other's deeply personal stories of their faith journeys. It is a place to begin to heal deeply entrenched and wounding divisions and seek together God's desired purposes in the world.

Rev. Wesley Granberg-Michaelson's latest book is "Without Oars: Casting Off into a Life of Pilgrimage." He serves on the International Committee of the Global Christian Forum and was General Secretary of the Reformed Church in America for 17 years. Learn more about Wes: wesgm.com

Learn more about the Global Christian Forum: howtohealourdivides.com/global-christian-forum/

«27»

How to Address the Asymmetry of Faith and Politics

Guthrie Graves-Fitzsimmons

I've spent my entire career battling a problem that is at the root of so much political and cultural division in our country. It's the simple yet profoundly wrong idea that the religious right and secular left are at odds in the public square. This couldn't be farther from the truth. The truth is that there are many areas of our collective life together that divide Americans. Across every issue area, there are a diversity of religious and secular opinions that animate people's views. Addressing this fundamental asymmetry in how we talk about faith and politics will help us heal our divides.

Consider gun violence prevention legislation. There is certainly a secular motivation for opponents of such legislation, whether that's the 2nd amendment of the United States Constitution or an appeal to the right to self-defense. Advocates of gun violence prevention legislation also argue from a non-religious standpoint, including the need to increase the use of background checks to prevent guns from getting into the hands of people who shouldn't have them. There is secular opposition and support for the legislation.

There are also religious appeals on both sides of this divide. Opponents of gun violence prevention legislation cite "God and guns" as two intertwined aspects of their identity that must be defended. Proponents say their advocacy reflects the God-given human dignity of all. Religious beliefs undergird both sides of this divide alongside the secular components.

The most common appearances of the secular left vs. religious right narrative come with abortion access and LGBTQ rights. It's often "God vs. Gays" and "God vs. Women" framing of these important issues. The religious opposition to abortion access and LGBTQ rights is well-known and pervasive in our culture. Yet there have been long-standing efforts by pro-LGBTQ and pro-choice activists who are motivated by their faith.

In my book, *Just Faith: Reclaiming Progressive Christianity*, I describe the work of the Clergy Consultation Service on Abortion. These ministers helped women seek out reproductive health care in the days before Roe v. Wade. Their work continues to this day as the Religious Coalition for Reproductive Choice. I also describe the long history of LGBTQ activism that was supported by religious leaders even before the Stonewall riots. This work for reproductive and LGBTQ justice is some of the most obscured religious activism in our public consciousness today. We tell stories of women and LGBTQ people fighting conservative religious people who want to oppress them. Yet the stories of these divides have the same secular and religious motivations on each side of the divide as the gun violence prevention issue I described earlier.

We must tell a better story about religion and how it intersects political, cultural, and social divisions. Religion is not the source of all good nor the advocate of all evil. When we can see how religious and secular motivations are at play in all of our divides today, we can see more clearly how to make progress together. There is no way to make any progress when we can't even acknowledge the factors at play.

I've been working at the intersection of faith and progressive politics for the past ten years. I've met so many incredible leaders doing work for the common good. On every issue we face today, whether issues of war and peace, immigration, climate change, ending poverty, education, or racial justice, there are faith-based advocates doing incredible work. I'm proud to call many of them friends and colleagues. I plan to spend the rest of my time walking this earth doing everything I can to support their work, contributing where I can to their efforts.

And yet, even though I'm deeply committed to building a more just and equitable world, I don't deny the religious motivations of people who are standing on the "other sides" of the divides we face. I've spent too much time with people I disagree with to write off their real convictions that are shaped by their life experiences and experiences with the divine. I don't call them "Fake Christians" or say they aren't truly acting in accordance with what they believe their faith teaches. There are hypocrites and liars in all corners, of course, who use religion as an excuse for advancing their own personal aims. But I truly believe that there are people who are shaped by their faith on all sides of our divides in society. It doesn't help anyone to ignore this reality.

When I talk about the asymmetry of faith and politics, a common question I get is, "How can I make a difference?" We can't all preach regularly about politics and religion or go on cable news and talk about the latest news of the day. I want to make this topic accessible for all readers, so here are three ways people can embrace this call to action in their own lives.

1. Get to know people on the "Other Side" of issues you care about.

We are wary of getting to know people with whom we disagree because doing so might somehow give the impression we are compromising on our values. This sadly prevents so many from understanding people they disagree with on important issues. Asking someone, "Why do you feel that way?" is not an endorsement of how they feel. You can instead find areas where you actually agree and at least understand the dynamics at play more. As a gay man, I can admit it has been difficult to get to know people on the "other side" of the debate over whether or not I'm deserving of the right to get married, adopt children, and not be fired from my job. It's difficult, but I would be kidding myself if I didn't acknowledge the deep religious convictions at play in the anti-LGBTQ movement. Hopefully, asking questions will also lead to sharing our own convictions. We might even find areas where we agree! It may also not be safe to actually talk to people, but we can understand different perspectives by reading and researching.

2. Acknowledge the history and reality of religion and religious people.

We must avoid the temptation to portray only people with whom we agree as true co-religionists. There is a long history of Christian activism in support of racial justice. That's true. But there is a shameful history of Christian support for slavery. That's also true. We can't look away from or deploy wishful thinking as we attempt to heal divides. Healing divides must always be grounded in truth and justice. Some people argue that bringing up the past distracts us from making progress in the here and now. I couldn't disagree more. Deciding to "look the other way" about gross injustice is a terrible foundation from which to try and heal. Reckoning with the past, including the many ways religion was used to harm others, does not condemn us to repeat that history. We can learn from the past, repent of our individual and collective complicity, and then move forward together with greater social cohesion.

3. Use your voice.

Each of us has the ability to influence people in our own social networks. We have a responsibility to share truthful information with our friends, family, and colleagues. No matter how small or large your social network is, you can use it for the common good. You can share articles about faith-based activism that might surprise people. You can comment or message friends who share misinformation. And you can shape the organizing movements and groups you're a part of already. If you're reading this book, I'm sure you're already involved in some non-profit organization, church group, or another form of working to create a better world. Raise your voice in this setting and address the asymmetry of faith and activism. Make sure your organization or church's work is acknowledging the faith-based motivations of people on all sides of our current divides. Together, we can create a stronger foundation for collective healing.

Guthrie Graves-Fitzsimmons is a fellow with the Faith and Progressive Policy Initiative at American Progress., and is the author of "Just Faith: Reclaiming Progressive Christianity." Learn more about Guthrie: americanprogress.org/person/graves-fitzsimmons-guthrie/

«28»

HEALING OUR INNER DIVIDES

Molly LaCroix

Healing divides requires engagement grounded in curiosity and compassion. We must be able to see the person on the other side of the issue, whatever it may be, in the fullness of their humanity. As obvious as this seems, if we are honest with ourselves, this is typically not our first response to someone whose opinion differs from ours. Rather than curiosity, we notice argumentativeness. Instead of compassion, we feel defensive. We find ourselves caught in the dilemma the Apostle Paul laments: "I do not understand what I do. For what I want to do I do not do, but what I hate I do" (Romans 7:15 NIV). This dilemma reveals our *inner divides*. Healing external divides requires us to heal our internal divides. If we ignore or suppress aspects of ourselves that we deem either unacceptable or too painful, we will not effectively engage in healing external divides. The Internal Family Systems (IFS) model provides a process for healing our inner divides.

As the name implies, the IFS model uses the metaphor of a family to understand human functioning. This metaphor recognizes what we notice when we attend to our inner experience: we are multiple. Consider one of the external divides you find most challenging to navigate. When you imagine discussing your views with someone on the other side of the issue, what do you notice? For example, you might have a part holding anger and another fearing doing or saying the "wrong" thing or provoking conflict. As inner conflict builds, you might notice a third part who steps in, silencing you. Challenging and complex issues elicit many different responses, often simultaneously. These dissonant reactions reflect our inner divides. When we are buffeted by conflicting impulses, it is difficult to engage productively with others holding opposing views. It is tempting to suppress the attitudes or reactions deemed "inappropriate," but this strategy does not heal our inner divides. Instead, the goal is to lead the inner family just as we would lead a team of people seeking the best outcome in an organization. Restoring effective leadership in our inner family enables us to glean the collective inner wisdom and resolve our internal conflicts, mirroring the desired result of efforts to heal external divides.

Let's take a closer look at the concept of an "inner family." As with any family, our inner family has different members with varying roles. The leader of the family reflects the image of God (see Genesis 1:27), with qualities such as compassion, curiosity, patience, perspective, and grace. These resources are intrinsic and cannot be eradicated, regardless of one's life experiences. We also have family members that provide unique qualities, talents, and characteristics. The ideal is a system with the leader and members working in harmony.

Of particular interest for the goal of healing divides, IFS recognizes the impact of adverse experiences on the inner family. Adversity takes many forms, including the more egregious issues of abuse, neglect, racism, and homophobia, as well as challenges such as financial insecurity, divorce, death of a parent or caregiver, and even multiple moves. None of us entirely escape adversity. As a result, some members of the inner family carry painful burdens, and other members take on jobs to protect us from the vulnerability of those burdens.

Adversity burdens our inner family members with painful emotions, distressing beliefs, disturbing images, and uncomfortable sensations. For example, an individual who experienced racism might hold shame, a belief that they are defective, images of scenes where they experienced racist remarks and actions, and tension in their gut or chest. These painful burdens threaten the system; thus, certain family members take on protective roles to suppress them by *exiling* the parts holding them.

Family members with protective roles, referred to as protectors, either proactively attempt to mitigate risks, or they reactively jump in to numb or distract us from pain when it surfaces. A person confronted by racism could have a protector who reactively confronts a person in anger to protect themselves from being overwhelmed by painful emotions. Or, a protector who fears escalating conflict could silence them. Conversely, the individual making a racist remark might have a protector who reacts with defensiveness to maintain the belief, "I am a good person" – another strategy to avoid the vulnerability of grief or shame for holding racist attitudes.

Both protectors and exiles require leadership grounded

in the intrinsic qualities we possess as bearers of the image of God. We do not want our interactions with others to be led by reactive or burdened inner family members. Restoring leadership of the inner family requires connecting with parts whose activity blocks our ability to engage constructively with others.

Dr. Richard Schwartz, the founder of the IFS model and the IFS Institute that promotes the model, is actively engaged in using IFS to promote healing across racial, political, and religious divides. Several years ago, he hosted a gathering of Arab and Jewish Israelis. In one session, an Arab man was paired with a Jewish woman. When it was the man's turn to share his experience, Dr. Schwartz first asked the Jewish woman to turn her attention inside to notice the parts of her that might be blocking her curiosity and compassion. A part of her wanted to share the impact of the holocaust on her family, rather than listening to the man's story. Dr. Schwartz prompted her to ask that part if it would be willing to step back and wait its turn so she could be fully present and open to hearing the man's story. Dr. Schwartz then asked the man what he noticed inside. He reported being aware of a protector who was "always" on duty, prepared to protect himself and his family. He said he was tired of the constant need to be vigilant and recounted events that reinforced the belief that he could never relax. Dr. Schwartz guided the man in connecting with this dedicated protector, so it felt appreciated.

Connecting with inner protectors is like developing any other relationship; we ask questions to learn about their role, motivation, and needs. When sufficient trust is established between the leader of the system and the protector, we ask, "What are you afraid would happen if you stopped doing what you are doing?" In this case, the protector showed the man a young boy inside who experienced a highly traumatic event. The man allowed the young boy (one of the exiled members of his inner family) to share his story. This is an essential component of healing, after which exiled parts can leave the time and place where adversity occurred. After sharing their story, these vulnerable parts of the system feel free to unload their burdens. They are restored to their original vitality, once again able to contribute their unique qualities to the inner family. As a result, protectors often relax and might even decide it is safe to give up their job, freeing additional members of the inner family to contribute their gifts to the system. The Jewish woman who witnessed this process felt deep compassion for the man; their tearful embrace was a vivid illustration of restored connection.*

In a recent article, Dr. Schwartz shared his experience using the IFS model to heal internalized racism. "I've been using IFS to work with the coalition of parts in well-meaning white people, including myself, that may interfere with the ability to face and act to change the ongoing damage that's been done to people of color."† With IFS, the perspective that a racist belief is held by a part of our inner family, and does not represent the totality of who we are, opens

---

* There is a video of this workshop available in the IFS Institute bookstore.
† Dr. Richard Schwartz, "Working with Internalized Racism," Psychotherapy Networker (Sept/Oct 2020). *https://www.psychotherapynetworker.org/magazine/article/2490/working-with-internalized-racism*

space for curiosity about why a part would hold those views. Rather than denying we have racist parts, IFS provides a roadmap for engaging with them and helping them heal. The reactivity white people feel when we hear terms such as "white privilege" or "white fragility" is a "trailhead," a signpost indicating there is territory to explore in our inner system.

Just as IFS is a powerful modality for helping white people explore internalized racism and the impact of privilege, it serves the Black community and other people of color in their journey of healing from racism. Requina Barnes, LICSW, a therapist and member of the Board of Directors of the IFS Foundation, shared her experience in using IFS both personally and with clients.* She identified several roles played by protective members of the inner family as a result of racism. One poignant example is a part that "feels like her race is switched off" when interacting with a majority white group because race is not usually acknowledged or discussed. It is easy to see the protective impulse driving a member of the inner family to suppress anything that it believes is unacceptable or attracts unwanted attention or criticism in majority-white settings. This type of protector is aware of situations where the individual felt shame or loneliness as an outsider in a group. Unless those burdens are healed and released, the protector will continue to work to homogenize an individual's personality and presence to feel safe. Ms. Barnes noted, "The protector makes sure the mask is on, and sometimes [the person] can't be authentic

---

* Personal communication.

anywhere." Our protective parts are fear-driven. The re-
ality-based fear in the Black community for physical and
emotional safety provokes the inner family members to be
vigilant about potential threats. If a person of color has experienced repeated injustice, their protectors will be front-
and-center in a dialog with a white person. The onus is on
the white person to work with their protectors so they can
engage with curiosity rather than defensiveness, accepting
whatever parts they notice in the other person's system
as well-intentioned and vital for their survival in a racist
culture. Deran Young, LCSW, founder of Black Therapists
Rock, stated, "When I first encountered [IFS], I felt like this
model was handcrafted for Black people because we have
so many things we've been forced to suppress."* The IFS Institute and the IFS Foundation are involved with several
initiatives to offer IFS training to people of color.

One of my colleagues shared another example of the
impact of IFS in healing divides. As a lesbian, she noticed
having protectors dedicated to managing her ability to fit in
and be safe in a majority heterosexual culture. Awareness
of our inner family members' influence is a significant first
step in healing divides, which she learned during her involvement in legalizing gay marriage in her state. The first
referendum failed, and she reports seeing individuals she
assumed were opposed to it (based on things such as political party or religious affiliation) as "enemies who betrayed
her" and fellow members of the LGBTQ+ community. She

---

*Comment made in a webinar featuring Dr. Richard Schwartz demonstrat-
ing the model with Deran Young, founder of Black Therapists Rock.

noted that the messages from the LGBTQ+ community during the first campaign were tinged with anger and criticism for anyone who was not supportive, clear evidence that their protectors were at the forefront. During the second campaign, she made an intentional effort to be authentic in her interactions with people she assumed were on the other side of the divide. Rather than allowing a protective part of her to manage her interactions to disguise her sexuality, she negotiated with the protector, so it allowed her to be authentic in connecting with people who had opposing views. Rather than looking at people through the eyes of a protector who was busy identifying safe and unsafe people and who was on her side versus the other side, she was able to draw on innate resources of courage and connection to build relationships. She is convinced that as she and others shifted from a protective stance to open engagement, the new relationships tipped the scales in favor of gay marriage in her state.

As these examples illustrate, attending to inner divides facilitates engagement in healing external divides. For information about exploring your inner family or training in the IFS model, see _https://ifs-institute.com/_. The IFS Foundation (_https://www.foundationifs.org/_) is engaged in research and other efforts to extend IFS beyond therapy to educators, organizations, and diverse communities. If you are interested in integrating IFS and Christian spirituality and applying the model to common causes of distress, please visit _mollylacroix.com/_

Molly LaCroix is a licensed marriage and family therapist (LMFT) in private practice. She received her master's degree in marriage and family therapy from Bethel Seminary San Diego and returned to Bethel as an adjunct professor in the MFT program. Learn more about Molly: mollylacroix.com/

«29»

To Create a Shared Future, Shift Whose Voices are Welcome at the Table

K Scarry

Beginnings.

Some time in late October 2020, my pastor called to ask if I could fill in for him and offer a sermon for the first week in November. It was an easy question to answer. The church: my most beloved space, my deepest community, and the place I find belonging; the place where I was given a handmade quilt when I was born; the place where I was the lead in the Christmas musical; the place I interned as a seminarian; the place that chose to ordain me. The answer: yes, I'll preach.

It did not dawn on either of us at the time that I'd be settling in behind the pulpit (well, music stand), only five days after the 2020 presidential election, one day after the news would report Joe Biden's win.

Four years prior, the 2016 election resulted in a Donald Trump victory, and the days after showed division throughout the United States the likes of which had not been seen in decades. This required reckoning: who had we become as a country? When did we forget how to talk to one another? Many of us were feeling the acute pain of polarization from our friends, family, neighbors, and community, and felt unsure what our next steps might be.

The People's Supper was borne out of those wrestlings and a desire to foster connection across difference. The three women who founded it were all already running their own nonprofits, focused on grief, faith-based social justice, and harassment, respectively. On the surface, they were wildly different from one another. But at the time, the founders and the communities they served found themselves in the same moment of reckoning that we as a country faced. Some members longed for a space to breathe, to acknowledge the profound sources of grief and fear that attended the election, and to hold one another. Others were seeking a way to understand, to break free of their filter bubbles, and to go beneath the headlines and to forge connection in place of its opposite. They began inviting people across the country to sit down for dinner with folks in their community who might not share their identities or ideological perspectives. All who joined were asked to agree on one thing: We were not going to argue our way out of this.

I joined the team soon after its inception. Four years after the first People's Supper, more than 10,000 people had sat around People's Supper tables in more than 100 communities across the country. More than that, we had all learned a thing or two about how to do the work of repair in our communities. Our work has remained focused on building trust and connection, but it didn't take long to realize the problem was not merely political polarization. We now work alongside community organizations to examine together: *What needs healing here?* Or, as I like to think about it: *What is the thing that keeps us from building a future here that works for all of us?*

As I prepared that sermon, I turned over every word, every letter, recalling the voices of countless people I had shared a meal with over the years, who might hear this sermon from different vantage points. Some would be coming to church that Sunday feeling an exhale. Some would arrive feeling an incredible sense of defeat.

I made my best attempts to offer a sermon that held truth, called us to work for justice, and did not choose one side over another. Still, my church received a letter. My pastor called to share the news. A long-time member cited my sermon as the reason she was leaving the congregation after more than 30 years. It felt clear to her that our church was heading toward "darkness" and "oppression."

I could stop there. That this woman was a long-time member of the congregation, and that my sermon was the thing that caused her to leave our church would be hard enough. But this woman was also my mom's dear friend, whose son I grew up with. This woman was — and remains — someone I call beloved to me, whose home was a haven when my parents needed someone to look after me. Her doors were always open to me. So her words were particularly piercing.

I know this work to be as much about our personal relationships as it is about our larger communities. I've been called by many a "bridge-builder," though I wrestle with the term. It's a complex role, if a rewarding one: trying to do the work of harm reduction in a society that is structur-

ally unequal, working to set up spaces where we are connecting people without retraumatizing those who are often
on the margins in our country, balancing the need for accountability, reckoning with consequences of our actions,
all while believing in people's capacity to grow. When I'm
in the throes of trying to repair the breach across lines of
difference, it helps me to remember that this work is, to use
Eugene Peterson's phrase, "a long obedience in the same direction."* This long obedience is a commitment to a vision
of a more just society and taking small steps towards that
society over and over again.

Friend, I meet you here. In the questions of what it
means to build communities of belonging and equity, in
the questions of how we might repair relationships across
lines of difference, and I meet you even in the moments of
wondering if it's possible. I join you as a fellow journeyer:
someone who believes in this work so deeply even on the
days where it's a struggle. This work is *a long obedience in
the same direction*, and we can travel together.

Erie.

We were working on a series of gatherings for people
across political lines in the weeks leading up to the mid-
term elections in 2018 when we got a call. A 2017 USA Today article had named Erie, Pennsylvania as the worst place
in the country for African Americans to live. The Mayor of
Erie reached out to The People's Supper wanting help. My
colleagues Jen Bailey, Margaret Ernst, and Lennon Flowers

---

*Eugene Peterson, *A Long Obedience in the Same Direction*

shared the initiative with me, inviting me to take the lead on it, which felt at the same time both daunting and hopeful. I agreed to take it on.

There were 80 participants: 20 African Americans, 20 Latinx, 20 New American Citizens, and 20 White participants. We embarked upon seven gatherings over six months. The first gathering was what we call a bridging supper, connecting all participants across lines of race and ethnicity. The next was an affinity supper, where we split participants into their racial or ethnic groups in order to give them a place to unpack the truths of their experiences from within those identities. This space, while seemingly counterintuitive to the overall mission, was integral in providing both deep self-examination and harm reduction in the series. White participants could examine whiteness: *When was the first moment you realized you were white? What's something related to race that you don't understand but don't feel comfortable bringing up?* Participants of color could build collective resilience and have some space to lament their experiences of racism in Erie: *Where does it hurt?*[*]

After the affinity gathering, we gathered for two more bridging suppers, where participants were led through a design thinking exercise to come up with ways to make Erie more equitable, inspired by the stories they had heard. Mayor Joe Schember had agreed to take on whatever initiatives were agreed upon, sharing his power with a group of residents who collectively looked a lot more like Erie than the city's leadership did. We then invited 300 Erie residents to

---

* Ruby Sales, *https://onbeing.org/programs/ruby-sales-where-does-ithurt/*

hear these ideas and make commitments to see them come to fruition, knowing it takes all of us to make real change.

Since then, Erie has launched two minority small business incubators, ensuring that immigrant- and BIPOC-owned businesses in town have the support and infrastructure they need to survive. They're working toward an Erie Promise scholarship, so that all Erie Public School students will have access to higher education. They have made sure that all Erie public works and public safety employees have completed a cultural competency training, and they have hired a diversity, equity, and inclusion consultant. The initial People's Supper participants are part of a council to the mayor's staff to help the whole community become more equitable.

A year prior to this series' close, a seminary professor of mine stood in the middle of our classroom and spoke. "That side is policy change," he said, pointing, before turning to point to the opposite wall, "and that side is relationship building." He looked out at us and challenged: "Plot yourself along this line: what do you think leads toward real change in our communities?" I remember the tension that overcame my body in that moment, and I remember that I did not have the language for the dissonance this question presented. Erie was the place where I'd learned that trust-building is a necessary part of systemic change, if you want those making the decisions to reflect the community. The work of trust-building is deeply linked to policy change and that for marginalized communities especially, conversation that leads to real action is the foundation of such trust. The work of The People's Supper in Erie was the start of our mission to accompany other communities in addressing racial inequities.

After our very first supper, an Erie participant pulled me aside. "I'm one of the people who is always asked to show up to find solutions to our city's problems, and not once have I been invited to get to know my neighbor first," they said. I was methodically stacking all the extra drinking glasses, my mind preparing for the debrief I'd have with the mayor's staff the next day, and this statement stopped me in my tracks.

You.
If you want to create a shared future, shift whose voices are welcome at the table.

You don't need to know all the people you are going to invite; you just have to know a few folks who are connected to diverse networks, and welcome each of them to be part of the inviting process. Pay attention: what does your community look like, and how can you ensure that your gatherings reflect that? As you're planning, your leadership needs to also reflect the group you're convening — any decision-points for the process at hand need to be made by folks who represent the larger group.

In racial justice work, make it a series, and offer affinity spaces.

Sitting down for one meal together will not do it. Gather over time, to let trust build amongst your participants. Be sure to include affinity spaces. People of color need some space to share their experiences of racism without risk of any white person's misunderstanding (no matter how well-meaning) or doubt. White folks need space to get honest with each other, too, and to flex the muscle of accompanying and interrupting each other in their unlearning.

Return to why you started, commit to the work over time, adjust as you go.

This is slow work. Trust-building is necessary to sustain you in whatever else you try to do together. Though we might be apt to start with solutions, instead begin by examining whose voices are not welcome at the table. Whose perspectives have we not considered? Who are we speaking for instead of welcoming in? Who has always been making the decisions for our community, and who is missing? Set a place for them. Keep clear on your mission, and adjust as you go. In Erie, we constantly had to remind ourselves why we started this work, and we had to continue on in the way we started – with a willingness to see the deeper stories of one another, to examine ourselves, and to believe better for Erie's future.

Finally.

In his welcome letter to all the participants in the Erie Supper series, Mayor Schember wrote this: *Tonight we are writing another important chapter. One that will make us a city that lives the American Dream, a city where age, race, ethnicity, religion, heritage, gender, sexual preference and even which side of State Street you live on become traits that unify us, rather than divide us. Let this process enable us all to see the value we each bring to this community; let us all*

celebrate the rich, diverse cultures that make us uniquely Erie.
Let us commit to the work, remembering that this is a long obedience in the same direction. Stay in it for the long game, taking small steps over and over again towards a more just world. Keep close at hand the vision with which you started. Continue to cultivate the relationships and trust necessary to build a shared future that works for all of us. Hold this work with humility and care, mindful of the truth that what you don't know far outweighs what you do. Engage with integrity, and adjust as you learn better. Know that we do not labor alone.

Want to get involved?

The People's Supper has distilled a number of our learnings over the years into a group of guidebooks, which can be found at *thepeoplessupper.org/resources*. These are free and accessible to anyone- and we offer them for communities all over the country to use towards repairing the breach in their interpersonal relationships. Feel free to use them as you seek to do this work in your community. If you are interested in a racial justice series with more ongoing support, or in having our coaching and thought partnership in a more hands-on way, reach out to *info@thepeoplessupper.org*.

K Scarry is Community Director of The People's Supper. She has worked in a number of non-profit organizations exploring different manifestations of community: with women coming out of sex trafficking, in a fraternity house, as an associate pastor, and as a chaplain in a maximum security women's prison. She' holds a Masters of Divinity from Wesley Theological Seminary. Learn more about K: thepeoplessupper.org/about-us

«30»

HOW MORMONISM
CAN SAVE AMERICA

Jana Riess

There's a controversial Mormon prophecy* that claims there will come a time when the United States Constitution will be hanging by a thread as fine as a single strand of silk, and the Mormon people will step in to save the nation from destruction. This is the infamous "white horse" prophecy, which gets trotted out every time a right-wing Mormon (Ammon Bundy, Glenn Beck) says or does something stupid or a Mormon is running for president.

It doesn't seem to matter how often or how soundly the Church of Jesus Christ of Latter-day Saints has refuted the white horse prophecy as having nothing to do with Mormon founder Joseph Smith. Although he made a few vague claims about Mormonism one day saving the nation, the full-on prophecy as we know it was not written until he'd been dead for nearly 60 years.

The Church denounced the prophecy at its October 1918 General Conference, saying it proceeded "out of darkness, concocted in some corner," and had not come "through the proper channels of the Church." The religion's

---

*_https://en.wikipedia.org/wiki/White_Horse_Prophecy_

president at that time, also named Joseph Smith (yes, we do know that is confusing) called the so-called prophecy "ridiculous" and "simply false; that is all there is to it."* Yet the prophecy persists in the Mormon American imagination; we Latter-day Saints seem to love the image of ourselves as saviors who swoop in at the eleventh hour to save the nation from itself.

Speaking for myself, I think the white horse prophecy is bogus. That doesn't mean that every part of it is BS, however. There is a way in which Mormons *can* save America from itself—and with every passing year, America needs that particular kind of salvation more and more.

Let me paint a picture. Right now, we live in a country in which it is entirely possible for liberals and conservatives to inhabit unprickable bubbles of their own design. Liberals get their news from CNN and MSNBC, while conservatives tune in to Fox News. Liberals log on to their self-selecting Facebook feeds and see outrage about how the Trump administration botched the coronavirus response, cozied up to Russia, exaggerated his administration's achievements, and rolled back environmental protections. Conservatives log on to *their* self-selecting Facebook feeds and share their outrage about Antifa, improper care of military veterans, and Trump not getting more credit for pre-pandemic job growth.

Politically, America has not been this divided in many decades, perhaps even since the eve of the Civil War. Since

---

* Don L. Penrod, "Edwin Rushton as the Source of the White Horse Prophecy," BYU Studies 49 no. 3 (2010), *https://byustudies.byu.edu/article/edwin-rushton-as-the-source-of-the-white-horse-prophecy/*.

the 1950s, the Gallup Organization has tracked public approval ratings of U.S. presidents by party. Back in the 1950s, a majority of Americans could legitimately say "I like Ike" and mean it: not only did 88% of the members of his own party approve of him, but 49% of Democrats did too.* What we see now, by contrast, is a country split right down party lines: in Donald Trump's America, on the eve of the 2020 presidential election, a stunning 95% of Republicans said they approved of the way he was running the country. Only 3% of Democrats could say the same.†

In other words, we used to have a political gap in this country of thirty or forty points separating Republicans and Democrats. In the Eisenhower example above, it was 39 percentage points. In Trump's America, *it was 92 points*, making him the most polarizing figure in modern political history.

Such hyper-partisanship shows little sign of abating even now that Trump is no longer in office. Republicans and Democrats are inhabiting completely different worlds.

And in most of the country, they attend religious congregations that reinforce their views. Over the past three decades, social scientists have tracked a remarkable re-sorting of Americans as Republicans have become more, and Democrats less, religious. In the 1970s, there was no "God gap" in American politics—members of both parties were more or less equally committed to faith. Now, though, Re-

---

* *https://news.gallup.com/poll/203006/obama-job-approval-ratings-politically-polarized-far.aspx*
† October 16–27, 2020 Gallup presidential approval ratings, *https://news.gallup.com/poll/203198/presidential-approval-ratings-donald-trump.aspx*.

publicans are not only more religious, but are a particular *kind* of religious, with growing numbers embracing a brand of conservative evangelical Protestantism. Churches become echo chambers, and those who don't agree with the politics preached from the pulpit become increasingly isolated. One study found that two-thirds of Republicans attended religious congregations where they felt that most of their fellow parishioners shared their political views. Only a quarter of Democrats had the same experience.* Not surprisingly given how lonely their experience with religion can be, a strong percentage of Democrats are leaving religion, which compounds the "God gap" even more.

I'm in my early 50s and can't remember a more politically and religiously divided time. In 2018, I voted a straight-party ticket for the first time in my life. I feel great despair at the way so many people in the Republican Party have abandoned their alleged Christian values to cast their lot with a fear-mongering narcissist.

But I find some hope in my own Mormon people. In my life, all the aforementioned echo chambers apply: where I get my news, for example, and what my social media looks like. Even the neighborhood I live in is largely reflective of my political views, judging from the yard signs I see come election time.

But all that fades away when I go to church, because in Mormonism I don't have a choice about the community I belong to.

---

*Michelle Margolis, *From Politics to the Pews: How Partisanship and the Political Environment Shape Religious Identity* (Chicago: University of Chicago Press, 2018), 143.

Mormons attend church based on geography, plain and simple. You don't get to congregation-shop based on which ward has the hippest bishop or the largest youth group (though some Mormons will actually hunt around in different wards *before* buying a house, knowing that once they move they'll be locked in to those ward boundaries). And you certainly don't get to choose where to go to church based on your political tendencies.

I used to rail against this policy, especially when I moved to a rural area where I knew no one and had little in common with the long-term residents of that ward. They were Kentuckians born and bred, and I was a carpetbagger, just passing through. Many hadn't finished college, and I'd just gotten my PhD. I was the only one with a John Kerry sticker on my car in the parking lot.

And yet in the seven years I lived there, something magical happened to me. I came to genuinely love them, and even laugh about our differences. I once pointed out to a woman in my book club that she had stenciled the Mormon hymn lyrics "peace and plenty here abide" right on top of the gun cabinet in her family room. She laughed too, saying she had never considered the irony. She baked me cookies for my birthday.

Back in those days, my Mormon ward was not the only place in my life where I regularly encountered—and loved—people whose views were diametrically opposed to mine. But I would say it is now. The worlds I swim in at work are primarily academia and journalism, both of which have a particular political persuasion. As I've said, our online interactions nowadays tend to merely reinforce

218

our thinking. If they don't, we all-too-quickly unfriend one another, often in ugly ways.

As a Mormon I don't get that option. In 2016, I noted with dread that a number of key members of my ward had Donald Trump signs in their yards. It was difficult for me to understand how they could be taken in by this man whose actions and values were so antithetical to the gospel we believed in. But because I knew and served alongside these people personally, I had a duty to *attempt* to understand. My bishop with the Trump sign was a salt-of-the-earth individual who spent Saturdays helping church members and even total strangers, raking their leaves and visiting them in the hospital. While many of my fellow liberals were denigrating Trump voters as dupes at best and evildoers at worst, there was my bishop, a Trump supporter who fit neither of those categories. Because of geography, I had to sit with that contradiction every Sunday. I think I emerged from it a better person. A better American.

Mormonism teaches me that I don't get to excommunicate folks from my world just because we disagree. And I am so, so glad of it. Being forced out of my comfort zone is – well, uncomfortable. But it's uncomfortable in an important way, as we become better in community with one another than we are when we can pretend the other side is anything less than human.

America needs that now more than ever before. So if there is a white horse prophecy in which my religion really does swoop in to save the nation, it will surely be because of this: Mormons have not yet given up on each other, and on the possibility of life together.

This essay has been expanded and adapted from the Religion News Service column "How Mormonism Can Save America," which was published on August 3, 2018 and is used with permission of Religion News Service; https://religionnews.com/2018/08/03/how-mormonism-can-save-america/.

Jana Riess is a senior columnist for Religion News Service and the author of many books, including "Flunking Sainthood" and "The Next Mormons." She has a PhD in American religious history from Columbia University.

«31»

THREE SHIFTS FOR HEALING
RELIGIOUS DIVIDES

Rabbi Rami Shapiro

Before we can take up the challenge of healing divides, we have to be clear as to why such divides exist in the first place. To put it bluntly: while diversity is inherent in nature, divides are narratives one is taught that elevate "the other" as an existential threat to one's privilege, power, and authority. As any preschool teacher will tell you, toddlers may fight over who gets to play with what toy, but they do not fight over abstractions such as race, color, religion, sex, and national origin. The only people who fight over these divisions are people who have been taught these divisions and indoctrinated to hate the "other" in light of them. The chief source of "othering" is religion.

Religious divides are systemic to parochial religions: religions that lay exclusive claim to truth. Healing religious divides means seeing through the illusory nature of such claims. This healing can happen when we make three substantive shifts in our thinking: shifting from belief to hypothesis; from metaphysics to metaphor; and from the parochial to the perennial.

Shifting from Belief to Hypothesis

Religious beliefs are ideas we hold to be true without any evidence outside the religion itself that they are, in fact, true. We inherit our religious beliefs from someone in whom we have invested authority: parents, clergy, teachers, etc. For example, as a child raised in an Orthodox Jewish household, I was taught by all three authorities that God, the creator of the universe, chose the Jews from among all the peoples of the earth to receive His (*sic*) one and only revelation (Torah), and to hold in perpetuity the deed to the Promised Land of Israel. The only evidence for this belief is the Torah itself. Because I was taught to believe that Torah was true, I came to believe the claims of Torah are true.

Such circular reasoning is at the heart of parochial religious thinking: thinking that confirms as true beliefs that are *a priori* thought to be true. This is why Christian theologians never discover that the Holy Trinity consists of Brahma, Vishnu, and Shiva rather than Father, Son, and Holy Spirit. And why Hindu devotees of Krishna never discover that there is no God but Allah. And why Muslims never discover that Moses not Mohammad was the greatest of God's prophets. And why Buddhists never discover the eternal and unchanging Atman/soul of the Hindu when doing so would violate the initial claim of Buddha that no such soul exists (anatman). When it comes to religion, we discover only what our religion allows us to discover, and what religion allows us to discover leads to divides that all too readily lead to fear, hatred, and violence.

Given that there is no objective evidence proving the truth of any religious belief, I suggest we shift from speaking of religious beliefs to religious hypotheses. A belief insists it is true. A hypothesis says it may be true, but to know for sure we must test it. Belief has no need for testing, and in fact is adamantly opposed to testing. Hypotheses welcome rigorous testing, or, if testing is not possible, encourage one who holds to the hypothesis to do so lightly knowing that it could very well be false.

Shifting from Metaphysics to Metaphor

Parochial religions think flat: valuing the literal over the figurative. When we think flat, we think stupid. When we think stupid, we cling to belief rather than open to hypothesis.

One of the best examples of flat thinking is C.S. Lewis's Trilemma. Lewis takes Jesus's claim literally, that "I am the way and the truth and the life. No one comes to the Father except through me" (John 14:6 NRSV). And then Lewis asks whether Jesus is a liar, a lunatic, or Lord when he makes this claim. From Lewis's point of view Jesus couldn't be a liar or a lunatic, so he must be Lord. Lewis' Trilemma isn't an invitation for testing a hypothesis but for affirming an already established belief. His Trilemma is rooted in rhetoric rather than reason.

Lewis's Trilemma has been presented to me many times, and my answer is always the same: I refuse to be limited to these three choices. Maybe Jesus is a poet or a mystic speaking metaphorically rather than metaphysically. Maybe Jesus isn't speaking from his ego at all but from his realization of the unity of all happening in the infinite Happening of God as Ehyeh, I AM (see Exodus 3:14). Maybe Jesus is saying, "I

AM is the way and the truth and the life, and only when you awaken as I AM can you realize your true nature as God and know that you too are the Way, the Truth and the Life." Or maybe Jesus never said these words at all.

Assuming for argument's sake that Jesus did say he was the Way, the Truth, and the Life, I hear him affirming what mystics from many traditions have affirmed. To cite but two: "I am the Truth" (Mansur Al–Hallaj, 858–922); "See now that I, even I, am God. God is I and I am God" (Abraham Abulafia 1240-1291). This realization of I AM as the source and substance of all reality shatters the flat thinking of Lewis's Trilemma and invites us to discover the truth of I AM for ourselves as ourselves.

Shifting from Parochial to Perennial

Religious divides are rooted in beliefs taken literally and held unquestioningly. Parochial religions perpetuates division because each insists that it and it alone is the one true religion. Eschewing honest investigation, parochial religions have only one way to prove their claim: slaughtering the adherents of other religions. Whenever this is possible in this life, parochial religions do not hesitate to engage in such slaughter. Whenever this is impossible in this life, parochial religions project the suffering of believers of other religions to some afterlife.

There is no hope for transforming parochial religion, but there is an alternative to them. At the mystic heart of parochial religion is Perennial Wisdom, a four–fold hypothesis affirmed by the great mystics throughout time and across cultures:

1. All life is the happening of nondual Aliveness called by
   different names: Brahman, YHVH, Allah, Mother, Tao,
   Dharmakaya, etc.
2. Human beings have the innate capacity to awaken in,
   with, and as this Aliveness.
3. Awakening to Aliveness reveals a universal ethic of justice and compassion rooted in the Golden Rule and de-
   voted to the ideal of being a blessing to all the families
   of the earth, human and otherwise (see Genesis 12:3).
4. Awakening to Aliveness and being a blessing comprise
   the highest calling of every human being.

This four-fold hypothesis of Perennial Wisdom invites
testing.

Testing our Hypothesis and Healing Our Divides

When you shift from belief to hypothesis, you live more
humbly. When you shift from metaphysics to metaphor,
you think more creatively. When you shift from parochial
to the perennial, you free yourself from all divides, seeing
self and other—all others—as unique and precious man-
ifestings of an infinite dynamic nondual Reality called by
many names (Krishna, Allah, Brahman, Kali, YHVH, God,
Tao, Mother, Dharmakaya, etc.) and captured by none.
And when you make these shifts, you see the many as the
One and the One as the many; differences abound but divides are shattered.

This assertion is itself a hypothesis in need of testing.
As the Buddha is thought to have said, "Do not believe in
anything simply because you have heard it. Do not believe
in anything simply because it is spoken and rumored by

many. Do not believe in anything simply because it is found written in your religious books. Do not believe in anything merely on the authority of your teachers and elders. Do not believe in traditions because they have been handed down for many generations. But after observation and analysis, when you find that anything agrees with reason and is conducive to the good and benefit of one and all, then accept it and live up to it."

How do you test the hypothesis of Perennial Wisdom? There are many ways, but I have found that the most direct path is Atma–vichara/Self–Inquiry as taught by Ramana Maharshi (1879–1950). Simply practiced, Self-Inquiry is the questioning of one's experience by asking oneself

"Who is thinking this thought?"

"Who is feeling this feeling?"

"Who is doing this action?"

Asking such questions reveals an "I" beyond the "I" of the thinker, feeler, and doer. This "I"—what Ramana calls I – and the Bible calls "I AM" and I call Aliveness—is pure awareness without race, color, religion, sex, national origin, or any other distinguishing label or form. It is the I AM beyond the "I, me, mine" of self yet includes the "I, me, mine" of self.

With the realization of I AM the divides that plague us are healed because the divisions they fuel are shattered. Without this awakening there is no healing.

Invitation: Walking the Path of Perennial Wisdom

An eight–day training in Perennial Wisdom is offered three times each year, based on the book "Perennial Wisdom for the Spiritually Independent." The goal of the retreat is realizing your true nature as a manifesting of the nondual Divine.

The retreat begins on a Sunday with the first five days taught through pre-recorded talks and an accompanying workbook exploring five questions central to the spiritual search for wisdom: Who Am I? Where Did I Come From? Where Am I Going (When I Die)? How Shall I Live? and Why? Each recording consists of three parts: an exploration of the question, a selection of Perennial Wisdom teachings from the world's religions that speak to the question, and a contemplative practice for finding the answer to the question. These sessions are pre-recorded, to allow you to work through the material at your own pace, and to listen to the lessons at your convenience as often as you choose.

Beginning on Friday evening we shift from pre-recorded sessions to live sessions via Zoom. Our two-hour Friday evening session focuses on creating community among the participants and answering questions regarding the five lessons just completed. Saturday and Sunday sessions take a deeper dive into the realization of your divine nature and the implications of that revelation for your relationships, persons, and the planet as a whole.

For more information on Walking the Path of Perennial Wisdom please visit _oneriverfoundation.org/_.

Rabbi Rami is a renowned teacher of spirituality across faith traditions, an award-winning storyteller, poet and essayist. His books include "The Sacred Art of Lovingkindness: Preparing to Practice," "Recovery–The Sacred Art: The Twelve Steps as Spiritual Practice" and "The Divine Feminine in Biblical Wisdom Literature: Selections Annotated & Explained." Learn more about Rabbi Rami: rabbirami.com/

The Peace Path Model
Bridging the Muslim/Christian Divide

Jeff Burns

Evangelical Islamophobic Minister

Some days, it is still hard for me to remember that I was a rabid Islamophobe who hated Muslims for over fifteen years. I wanted nothing to do with Muslims, and I believed, like many other Americans, that they were intrinsically evil people. After a deep inner struggle, seeking God, and personal study, I began to see them in a different light. Still, I was unwilling to move towards them in love, reconciliation, and friendship.

Omar Leads Me Back to God

In February of 2005, I was having coffee at Starbucks on Creedmoor Road in Raleigh, North Carolina. I was deeply struggling about my new insights on Muslims and Islam, and I knew I had to resolve it. I prayed for God to give me a sign so clear I would never doubt that he wanted me to build bridges of love and peace between Muslims and Christians.

Approximately a minute later, a little Muslim boy came to my table (uninvited) and said, "Sir, my name is Omar, I am five years old, and I am here to teach you some Arabic." Omar was my sign from God.

For the next thirty minutes, Omar tried to teach me the Arabic alphabet, and after my encounter with this precious Muslim child, all my hate for Muslims was gone, and God filled my heart with His love for these beautiful people that I once feared and hated. My Islamophobic days were over. That day was the moment in time that I became a peacemaker and bridge builder. I never looked back.

From Islamophobic Evangelical to Peacemaker

My peacemaking journey has taken me all over the U.S. and to other nations. God has granted me great favor with many Muslims and Christians. Unfortunately, my most significant conflict point has not come from the Muslim community; instead, it has come from my tribe, the Christian church.

I was an early pioneer as an Evangelical peacemaker in the United States. Other Christian traditions had been practicing peacemaking and interfaith work, but I could not find models to follow in my faith tradition. I realized I had to create a model to train others based on my successes and failures. Over time my model came to be known as The PEACE PATH Model. It is a short practical guide for Muslims and Christians to reach out to each other and become friends. The sixty-page short version of the PP Model has been downloaded for free by many Muslims and Christians who want to create a better world. Several years ago, one of my friends, Dr. Michal Meulenberg, helped me take all that I was doing and organize it around this acronym. I will forever be grateful for her help.

What Is the PEACE PATH Model?

My model is a practical way for Muslims and Christians to choose to reject fear and to love one another. I based the PEACE PATH Model on a simple acrostic.

P – Participate In God's Dream For The World

E – Express God's Love

A – Advocate For the Common Good

C – Communicate God's Message of Reconciliation In Word & Deed

E – Experience Hospitality

P – Plant Peacemaking Communities

A – Apply the Five Practices

T – Team Up For Service Projects

H – Have People Over For Dinner

For the sake of time and space, I will boil the model down to its theological core message and the five core practices that give the model teeth so anyone can follow The PEACE PATH.

The Core Theological Message

The core message of Jesus (Isa)* is the foundation of the PP Model. Jesus said all the scriptures hang on two great

---

*In the Qur'an Jesus is called Isa Al Masih eleven times. Isa is the Arabic name for "Jesus" and "Al Masih" is Arabic for the Messiah (Al-Nisa 4:172). Approximately 100 versus refer to him. The Qur'an teaches that in order to be on the "Straight Path" (submitted to Allah) one must follow, fear, and worship God and obey Jesus or "Isa" (Az-Zukhruf 43:61-63 and Aal Imran 3:42-56).

commandments and the Golden Rule, exemplified in His Sermon on the Mount.

"You shall love the Lord your God with all your heart, love your neighbor as yourself, treat other people the way you want to be treated, and if you find enemies (or perceive them to be enemies), do everything within your power to make them your friends."

Martin Luther King, Jr. once said *The only way to get rid of an enemy permanently is to make him your friend.*

138 Islamic scholars met in Jordan in 2007 to confirm that they could find common ground with Christians based on this message. This initiative came to be known as *A Common Word Between Us and You.*

As I engage in peacemaking or peacebuilding between Muslims and Christians, this core message is where I begin. Jesus (Isa) PBUH* and Muhammad (PBUH) agree that this primal theological essence is for all people regardless of faith or religion. Our religious ideas and practices must lead us to work for the Common Good. As the Prophet Muhammad said in his Covenants, *"What's good for the Christian is good for the Muslim."* From God's view, Muslims and Christians have a symbiotic relationship.

---

* PBUH is an acronym for "Peace be unto him." Whenever a Muslim writes the name of prophets like Jesus (Isa), Moses or Muhammad they are to put (PBUH) after the prophets name. This is a sign of respect and honor to the prophet and their message. If a Muslim is giving a sermon or talking about a prophet she is supposed to say, "Peace be unto him." There is an interesting fact I have discovered about Jesus (Isa) in the Qur'an. He is the ONLY prophet that spoke peace upon himself. He is unique figure in the Qur'an (Maryam 19:33). It is also interesting to note that the Surah or chapter called "Maryam" is named after the Virgin Mary. Mary is the only woman mentioned by name in the Qur'an. She is also deeply revered because she was virtuous and the mother of Jesus.

The Five Practices

A theological idea has no relevance without practices that can bring it to life and help others. As a result, I discovered five practices that I keep doing wherever I go that align with the core message.

1) How can I be a blessing to you and your community? Whenever I become engaged with the Muslim community, this is the first thing I ask them. If Muslims think I am sincere, they will answer the question. Some have asked my friends and me to help them do projects at the mosque, tutor in English, move from dialogue to friendship and support their young people who might be struggling. The response is endless. We ask Muslims what they need, not what we think they need.

2) Become good friends without a hook or agenda. I started an intentional community that focused on these five practices, and they developed strong love and trust with their Muslim friends.

3) Eat together. When I train individuals, both Muslims and Christians, I tell them we have to go beyond dialogue and become friends. We are not becoming friends until we are eating in each other's homes and our children are playing together. One of the biggest challenges is training Christians to serve only *Halal* or *Kosher* food to their Muslim friends. Once Muslims know you will do only these types of meals, they will gladly come to your house for dinner

4) Explore Faith Together. As we become friends, we can begin to discuss our differences and commonalities. This faith exploration is not a time for benign religious discussions nor polemics or apologetics, but to let the other teach us to understand and vice versa. As a result of serving them, becoming friends, eating together, exploring faith in friendship, we had Jesus Dialogues at the mosques, churches, and universities. The MSA (Muslim Student Association) sponsored our Jesus Dialogues at two different universities.

We also formed Communities of Reconciliation (COR) which were co-led by Muslims and Christians. They met and took a journey together for six months to a year together to become friends and break down the walls of prejudice, fear, and misunderstanding. They shared their life stories, favorite verses from their holy scriptures and asked each other questions. I have the curriculum for COR's in my PEACE PATH Model ebook. The results were terrific.

5) Do a service project together. Each COR group was ending their journey by doing a local humanitarian or service project. Some built Habitat Homes together; others worked for a weekend at the Ronald McDonald House at Duke Hospital to serve families who stayed there while their loved ones were in the hospital. Some groups fed the homeless together or served in community gardens to supply the local food banks.

We repeatedly affirmed the core message and did the five practices. This simple peace model has spread around the world. These practices are the way we participated in God's Dream for the world. We believed the Mission of God begins with friendship, and then we found out where God is working in our communities (His Dream), and we joined Him in that Dream through the five practices.

Over the past fifteen years, I discovered that Jesus' path of peacemaking and reconciliation is both *knowable* and *doable*. Through intentional friendship, meal-sharing, and listening, I've seen firsthand how former enemies can taste God's peaceable Kingdom, *right* here and *now*.

I get many messages from both Muslims and Christians who are using my peace model. Here are just a couple of samples among many.

A Christian Peace Practitioner

Hey Jeff,

I just wanted to write you to thank you for your trip several years ago to Sydney, Australia. I was profoundly impacted by that week, especially by your sharing, and since then, I have made many small efforts to bring Christians and Muslims together here in Australia.

The more significant thing I'm doing now is that I've created a two-day camp based on a lot of your PEACE PATH model used in very extreme communities in Indonesia, in Islamic universities, and with Islamic leaders. It is multiplying itself out into many different islands and communities.

Thanks again for your willingness to come "Down Under." It's still producing fruit and multiplying.

I hope to catch you some time along the way. There are invitations from Muslims for us to do this in Bangladesh, India, Nepal, and Tunisia, so who knows if Sudan might end up on the list as well.

Blessings.

Jack

A Muslim Peace Practitioner

Dear Dr. Jeff,

AsSalaamu Alaikum:

Grateful for your time and effort, Jeff; you have to know that you are making a difference in the way people view each other.

If only more people could hear your message.

The world needs it right now.

While we all say everyone is entitled to their opinions, the truth is, we loath each other for our opinions sometimes to the extent that we forget we're all brothers and sisters in this world on a journey back to Eden.

Hopefully, our intentions and deeds are accepted, and we don't find ourselves elsewhere. Your message (PEACE PATH Model) reminds us that we need help and not hinder one another with pointless bickering.

I've adopted your method (PEACE PATH Model), and as a Muslim, I've started to see the Bible and Quran are testaments of the same faith from the one God.

The devil is in the details. Our Holy Books tell us our intention judges actions.

Just a quick message to tell you your Message (PEACE PATH Model) is traveling, and you are now my Christian minister!

I pray God's peace and blessing upon you and your household.

Ameen.

Muhammad

These are only a small sampling of how Muslims and Christians are using the PEACE PATH Model. It has caused a "butterfly effect." Omar's story has been viewed, read, or heard by over 500,000 people; maybe more. Then they take the PEACE PATH Model and start applying this simple message of love and forgiveness to Muslims and Christians in their communities.

Would you like to join me on the Peace Path?

The PEACE PATH Model ebook:
https://mailchi.mp/d217a901a836/thepeacepath.

The PEACE PATH Model ebook on Paste.com: https://www.pas-temagazine.com/noisetrade/books/jeffburns/the-peace-path-a-practi-cal-manual.

Jeff Burns YouTube Channel I Follow The Path:
https://www.youtube.com/c/JeffBurnsThePath.

Jeff Burns is a peace and human rights activist. He has been active in building bridges of reconciliation, peacemaking, and friendship between Muslims and Christians in the U.S. and overseas. Jeff previously served as the East Coast Regional Director for Peace Catalyst International. Learn more about Jeff: jeffburns.org/.

EPILOGUE

Here I Raise My Ebenezer

Adam Thomas

You've just read dozens of stories of people and organizations engaged in the transformative work of healing our divides. One or two or a dozen of these essays lit the flames of your heart's longing to be a repairer of the breach, an active presence of reconciliation in this divided world. I would wager the fire ignited within you because the work described in these pages touched that place inside you where your deep gladness met the world's deep hunger, Frederick Buechner's famous definition of a calling.

Along with a refreshed ignition of your own call into God's mission of healing and reconciliation, I hope these pages blazed some new neural pathways in your mind. For one of the best ways to heal divides is to think new thoughts, and these pages certainly contain much that is thought-provoking. We read about myriad practices to speak across difference and to become more integrated within ourselves. We read about dozens of organizations making a positive impact on this world. We read...and now it is our turn to act.

I invite you to start with your own thoughts and with the

words you choose to order them. With all the new thoughts gained from this book jostling for places in your mind, take a prayerful moment to integrate their words with your own and allow those words to enliven you with renewed purpose.

The Word of God in the Hebrew Scriptures was a living, dynamic force. It wasn't a static thing people read or heard. The Word was an encounter. In English this gets rendered as "The Word of the Lord came to So-and-So Prophet." But what it really says is that the Word *happened* to the Prophets. The Word of God caught them up in its power and gave them words of justice and reconciliation.

Words shape worlds, and words shape thoughts. The last verse of my favorite hymn begins, "*Here I raise my Ebenezer / hither, by thy help, I've come.*" The *Eben Ezer* was the stone that Samuel set up to commemorate God's help in the Israelites victory over the Philistines. *Eben Ezer* means "stone of help." When we sing about raising our stones of help, we set ourselves within the same story that Samuel was telling about God. And we prayerfully imagine our way into the reality of God's constant presence and faithfulness. Now, if you sang that song out of the hymnal of my church, the Episcopal Church, you'd notice the word "Ebenezer" is missing. The verse begins with a rewrite: "Here I find my greatest treasure." While this thought is fine, it doesn't link at all to the next words: "hither, by thy help, I've come." Treasure-seeking is not the point of the hymn. The point of the hymn is recognizing our helplessness on our journey and God's inspirational blessing that helps our hearts tune to the resonance of God's presence. You see what happens when you change just a single word. Meanings change, get distorted.

Words matter.

The words we choose to employ shape the kinds of thoughts we *allow* ourselves to think. If the only way my spouse and I praised our daughter was by calling her "cute" or "pretty" or "sweet," we would not be contributing at all to her self-identifying as "strong" or "brave" or "independent." Of course I think my daughter is about the cutest person in the world, but I desire so much more for her than to box herself in over concerns about physical appearance. Society-at-large is going to handle that just fine, so the words we use to praise her must serve as a counterweight to that societal expectation.

Words define the parameters of our thoughts. One of the best ways to blaze new cognitive trails is to name a new idea with a word. There's the old joke that college professors like to make up words, which makes sense when you consider they're also trying to come up with new thoughts. When writing my book *Digital Disciple* way back in 2010, I needed a word to describe teens ignoring everyone at a party because they were glued to their devices. They weren't being antisocial; they were being "trans-social." That is, they were being social, just not with the people physically nearby.

Dr. Seuss made up words all the time in his children's books, and not just to make rhyming easier. In *The Lorax*, he describes a hose as "snergelly." Of course, it's not a "real" word, but you know exactly what it means when the Once-ler drops it down to share his story. When my kids started playing with LEGOs, they described a hose piece as "snergelly." For them, it is a real word, and their minds have invested it with meaning.

Once an idea has a name, we can all talk about it and awaken those new neural paths. Until I heard the word "cisgender," I had no idea I had a place on the spectrum of gender identities. Now that I know that word and understand the concept it represents, I see people who are not cisgender as part of that same spectrum and not as a nebulous (and perhaps frightening) other.

Not only do new words create new thoughts, but the ways we combine and curate the words we use serve to narrow or expand our minds. Instead of saying, "The blind," you can say, "a person who is blind," thus putting the person in front of their ableness. Or think about the language you hear when the news or statistics talk about the horrible reality of rape.

"A woman was raped last night on campus."

"Violence against women."

Nowhere in normative phrases like these do the perpetrators of rape appear. By constricting our language like this, we fashion rape as a "women's problem." But what if we reconceived these phrases with both parties to the violation?

"A man raped a woman last night on campus."

"Men acting violently toward women."

Now we have a new set of thoughts in our heads that our commonly used terms don't allow us to think. And while I will never include myself in the subset of men who engage in the crime and violation of rape, I am included in the full set of men who can work to lessen the patriarchal culture that allows rape to flourish and victims to feel ashamed of their own abuse.

We can apply this same logic to racial injustice in the United States. We can challenge the vast lexicon of terms like "thug" and "welfare queen," which unfairly stereotype African Americans. We can even change our own views of history by changing the words we use to describe it. Three examples have hit me hard and compelled me to change my own understanding of the history of the United States.

First, encouraged by reading Black authors, I no longer use the words "slavery" and "slave." Instead, I follow their lead and use the words "enslavement" and "enslaved." The word "slave" conjures up an identity for a person, as does the word "master." One is surely inferior to the other, hence their use to perpetuate the system. But calling those same people "enslaved person" and "enslaver" changes the narrative and removes the notion of superiority for the white "master." Now the "enslaver" is engaged in an evil business, and the "enslaved person" is still a person no matter the condition of their bondage.

Second, after a trip to The Legacy Museum and the National Memorial for Peace and Justice in Montgomery, Alabama, I changed the words I use when I write about lynching. Before the trip, I conceived of lynching as isolated attacks on people of color by a small number of white supremacists over a period of decades. But the Equal Justice Initiative, which created both the museum and the memorial, adds the words "racial terror" in front of "lynching." By framing the history of lynching with these words, I could now see what I could not before. Racial terror lynching was a system of control over the Black masses, in which white people killed over 4,000 Black people and terrorized millions more into submission. This racial terror was one of the main factors for "The Great Migration," in which six million Black people left the South in the first half of the 20th century.

Third, on the same trip, the Equal Justice Initiative helped me change my words, and thus my thoughts, about the Civil Rights Movement. I had always conceived of the people of the Civil Rights Movement fighting against segregation and going to jail in countless droves to protest unjust systems. And while this is true, a shift in perspective opened up the other side of history for me. Because the Supreme Court had decided several cases in favor of integration, Civil Rights workers actually had the law of the United States on their side. But local officials chose to ignore those laws in favor of state and local statutes which the highest court in the land had struck down. Thus, the ten years in the middle of the 20th century was a period of "resistance to integration." These new words helped me see the perpetrators of crimes were local governments and police, not the people they were arresting.

These shifts in language have changed how I conceive of American history. My white mind had fallen into a bad pattern: seeing "slave" as a full identity, downplaying lynching, and indicting the wrong people during the Civil Rights Movement. By changing just a few words, my thoughts have changed and expanded to see a different and clearer charting of our shared history.

EPILOGUE

I hope this book has changed and expanded some of your thoughts as you prepare yourself to heal our divides. God blessed Abraham and Sarah to be blessings in this world. May God bless you, too, granting you the grace to be a repairer of the breach, an active presence of reconciliation in this divided world.

Raise your *Eben Ezer*, for hither by God's help we've come this far. And with God's help, we will go much farther, healing our divides together.

The Rev. Adam Thomas is one of the editors of this volume and author of over a dozen books and curricula. You can find him at adamthomas.net and wherethewind.com.

Appendix

Links to Featured Organizations

3Practices: *3practicecommons.com*

The Absalom Jones Center for Racial Healing: *centerforracialhealing.org*

Arrabon: *arrabon.com*

The Better Arguments Project: *betterarguments.org*

The Center for Courage and Renewal: *couragerenewal.org*

The Center for Native American Youth: *aspeninstitute.org/programs/center-for-native-american-youth*

Church of the Holy City: *holycitydc.org/*

The Colossian Forum: *colossianforum.org*

Combatants for Peace: *cfpeace.org*

Corrymeela Community: *corrymeela.org*

Dinner Church: *dinnerchurchmovement.org*

Global Christian Forum: *globalchristianforum.org*

Honor the Earth: *honorearth.org*

Internal Family Systems Institute: *ifs-institute.com*

Institute for Justice and Reconciliation: *ijr.org.za*

The Julian Way: *neighboringmovement.org/the-julian-way*

Matthew 25/Mateo 25: *matthew25socal.org*

Narrative 4: *narrative4.com*

Native Wellness Institute: *nativewellness.com*

One River Foundation: *oneriverfoundation.org*

The Parents Circle – Families Forum:
theparentscircle.org/en/about_eng

Peace Catalyst International: *peacecatalyst.org*

The People's Supper: *thepeoplessupper.org*

Red Letter Christians: *redletterchristians.org*

Roots of Justice: *rootsofjusticetraining.org*

St. Andrew United Methodist Church: *gostandrew.com*

SEVOTA: *peaceinsight.org/en/organisations/sevota/*

Telos: *telosgroup.org*

Vote Common Good: *votecommongood.com*

White Bison *whitebison.org*

Links to Contributors

David M. Bailey: *arrabon.com*

Diana Butler Bass: *dianabutlerbass.com/*

Amy Julia Becker: *amyjuliabecker.com/*

Martin Brooks: *peacecatalyst.org/martinbrooks*

Dr. Jeff Burns: *jeffburns.org/*

Tiffanie S. Chan: *arrabon.com*

Shane Claiborne: *shaneclaiborne.com/*

Shannon Crossbear: *linkedin.com/in/shannon-cross-bear-329ab712/*

Lyn Cryderman: *writingforyourlife.com/lyn-cryderman/*

Todd Deatherage: *telosgroup.org/who-we-are/#team*

Dr. Calenthia Dowdy: *fight.org/fight-staff/calenthia-dowdy/*

Rev. Mark Feldmeir: *markfeldmeir.com*

Makoto Fujimura: *makotofujimura.com/*

Wes Granberg-Michaelson: *wesgm.com*

Guthrie Graves-Fitzsimmons: *americanprogress.org/person/graves-fitzsimmons-guthrie/*

Erik Gross: a*speninstitute.org/our-people/erik-gross/*

Michael Gulker: *colossianforum.org/about-us/team/*

Jim Hancock: *3practicecommons.com/our-story*

Rev. Justin Hancock: n*eighboringmovement.org/the-julian-way*

Jim Henderson: *3practicecommons.com/our-story*

Seth Henderson: *aspeninstitute.org/our-people/seth-henderson/*

Molly LaCroix, LMFT: *mollylacroix.com*

Brian D. McLaren: *brianmclaren.net/*

Michael McRay: *michaelmcray.com/*

Catherine Meeks: *centerforracialhealing.org/about*

Parker J. Palmer: *couragerenewal.org/parker/*

Jana Riess: *janariess.com/*

Rev. Brandan Robertson: *brandanrobertson.com/*

247

Vanessa Ryerse: _vanessaryerse.com/_

Rev. Dr. Alexia Salvatierra: _fuller.edu/faculty/alexia-salvatierra/_

K Scarry: _thepeoplessupper.org/about-us_

Rabbi Rami Shapiro: _rabbirami.com/_

Rev. Rich Tafel: _linkedin.com/in/richtafel_

The Rev. Adam Thomas: _adamthomas.net_

Frank A. Thomas: _drfrankathomas.com/_

Michael W. Waters: _michaelwwaters.com/_

Recommended Reading

Books from Our Featured Voices and Organizations

Freeing Jesus: Rediscovering Jesus as Friend, Teacher, Savior, Lord, Way, and Presence - by Diana Butler Bass

White Picket Fences: Turning toward Love in a World Divided by Privilege - by Amy Julia Becker
   Head, Heart, and Hands: An Action Guide - in PDF, eBook, and Audiobook formats

Jesus for President: Politics for Ordinary Radicals - by Shane Claiborne and Chris Haw

A House Divided: Engaging the Issues Through the Politics of Compassion - by Mark Feldmeir

Culture Care: Reconnecting with Beauty for Our Common Life - by Makoto Fujimura

Without Oars: Casting Off into a Life of Pilgrimage - by Wes Granberg-Michaelson

Just Faith: Reclaiming Progressive Christianity - by Guthrie Graves-Fitzsimmons

The Julian Way: A Theology of Fullness for All of God's People - by Justin Hancock

3 Practices for Crossing the Difference Divide - by Jim Henderson and Jim Hancock

Restoring Relationship: Transforming Fear into Love Through Connection - by Molly LaCroix

Peace Catalysts - by Rick Love

Faith After Doubt: Why Your Beliefs Stopped Working and What to Do About It - by Brian McLaren

I Am Not Your Enemy: Stories to Transform a Divided World - by Michael McRay

Living into God's Dream: Dismantling Racism in America - by Catherine Meeks

A Hidden Wholeness: The Journey Toward an Undivided Life - by Parker J. Palmer

Healing the Heart of Democracy: The Courage to Create a Politics Worthy of the Human Spirit - by Parker J. Palmer

The Next Mormons: How Millennials Are Changing the LDS Church - by Jana Riess

True Inclusion: Creating Communities of Radical Embrace - by Brandan Robertson

Faith-Rooted Organizing: Mobilizing the Church in Service to the World - by Alexia Salvatierra and Peter Heltzel

Perennial Wisdom for the Spiritually Independent: Sacred Teachings - by Rabbi Rami Shapiro

249

Digital Disciple: Real Christianity in a Virtual World - by Adam Thomas

How to Preach a Dangerous Sermon - by Frank A. Thomas

Something in the Water: A 21st Century Civil Rights Odyssey - by Michael W. Waters

Additional Recommended Reading

Defeating the Toxic New Normal, Finding Our Path Back to Empathy and Understanding - by Mike Burkhard

Race in America: Christians Respond to the Crisis - Laura Cheifetz and David Maxwell, eds.

Good White Racist? Confronting Your Role in Racial Injustice - by Kerry Connelly

Red State Christians: Understanding the Voters Who Elected Donald Trump - by Angela Denker

White Fragility: Why It's So Hard for White People to Talk About Racism - by Robin DiAngelo

Holy Chaos: Creating Connections in Divisive Times - by Amanda Henderson

The Hundred Story Home - by Kathy Izard

White Too Long: The Legacy of White Supremacy in American Christianity - by Robert P. Jones

How to Be an Antiracist - by Ibram X. Kendi

Jesus and John Wayne: How White Evangelicals Corrupted a Faith and Fractured a Nation - by Kristin Kobes Du Mez

Praying with Our Feet: Pursuing Justice & Healing on the Streets - by Lindsey Krinks

Designed to Heal: What the Body Shows Us about Healing Wounds, Repairing Relationships, and Restoring Community - by Jennie McLaurin and Cymbeline Tancongco Culiat

Undivided: A Muslim Daughter, Her Christian Mother, Their Path to Peace - by Patricia Raybon and Alana Raybon

The World is About to Turn: Mending a Nation's Broken Faith - by Rick Rouse and Paul O. Ingram

Becoming Brave: Finding the Courage to Pursue Racial Justice Now - by Brenda Salter McNeil

The Tyranny of Merit: What's Become of the Common Good? - by Michael J. Sandel

With Liberty & Justice for Some: The Bible, the Constitution, and Racism in America - by Susan K. Williams Smith

How to Fight Racism: Courageous Christianity and the Journey Toward Racial Justice - by Jemar Tisby

Copyrights

The essay on pages 91-97 is from *Culture Care* by Makoto Fujimura. Copyright © 2017 by Makoto Fujimura. Used by permission of InterVarsity Press, P. O. Box 1400, Downers Grove, IL 60515. *www.ivpress.com*.

Disclaimer

Although the authors have made every effort to ensure that the information in this book was correct at press time, the authors do not assume and hereby disclaim any liability to any party for any loss, damage, or disruption caused by errors or omissions, whether such errors or omissions result from negligence, accident, or any other cause. This book should not be construed as legal, therapeutic, or financial advice. If you would like to report an error, or request permission to reprint an excerpt from the book, please contact us at *https://howtohealourdivides.com/*. The opinions expressed in this book do not necessarily represent those of any other contributor or organization featured in this book.

Acknowledgements

Brian Allain

First and foremost, I would like to thank all of the outstanding contributors to this book, not only for that contribution, but more importantly for all the incredibly positive work they do to heal divides. In particular I would like to thank Adam Thomas for partnering to quickly create this book.

I would also like to thank our endorsers, all the members of our book launch team, and others who have supported this and our other efforts.

There is no way I could have developed this project, as well as the many other crazy things I do, without the strong, close, and never-ending support of my wife and lifelong partner Nancy Allain.

But above all I would like to thank you, our customer, who not only purchased this book, but more importantly, contributes in whatever ways you can to make the world a better place, both today and for generations to follow.

Adam Thomas

When Brian Allain approached me about partnering on this project, I wanted to say, "Yes," right away both because I would get to work with Brian and because we'd be helping to put something life-giving out into the world. But I was hesitant at the tight schedule and the scope of the project. Thankfully, Brian is a great partner, and he only needed to nudge me a tiny bit to agree. I'm so glad he did, as I feel blessed to have gotten to learn so much about so many transformative organizations in working on this project. Thank you, Brian.

I am grateful to all our contributors for their inspiring words and their timeliness in sending in their essays, which gave me the space to edit and design the book within a fairly short window. I'd particularly like to thank Brian McLaren, who encouraged me as my thesis advisor in seminary back in 2008 and helped set me on the path that led to my involvement in this book.

Finally, I'd like to thank my twin first-graders, who gave me time to sit at the computer when I wasn't working at church in order to work on the book, and my spouse Leah for being the most wonderful and supportive life partner I could ask for or imagine. Thanks be to God!

Brian Allain founded and leads *Writing for Your Life*, a resource center for spiritual writers, *Publishing in Color*, a conference series intended to increase the number of books published by spiritual writers of color, *Compassionate Christianity*, an online resource center for progressive Christians, and *How to Heal Our Divides*. Previously Brian served as Founding Director of the Frederick Buechner Center where he led the launch of Mr. Buechner's online presence and established several new programs and strategic partnerships. All of this is a second career, coming after many business and technology leadership positions in high-tech. Brian has an MBA from the Wharton School of Business at the University of Pennsylvania, where he was designated a Palmer Scholar, their highest academic award.

Adam Thomas wears many hats: pastoring an Episcopal Church in southeastern Connecticut, editing and designing books for independent writers, writing fantasy novels, podcasting about Jesus and nerdy stuff, and playing lots of Dungeons and Dragons. Adam published four books and curricula with Abingdon Press from 2011 to 2014 (*Digital Disciple, Letters from Ruby, Converge: Who is Jesus?*, and *Unusual Gospel for Unusual People*). When the twins were born in 2014, he switched to writing fantasy. You can find hundreds of sermons on _wherethewind.com_ and several fantasy novels on _adamthomas.net_.

Printed in Great Britain
by Amazon

61584829R00161